Do not be afraid,
little flock,
for your Father
delights to
give you the kingdom.
(Lk. 12:32)

the
# Community
of the
# King

## Howard A. Snyder

INTER-VARSITY PRESS
DOWNERS GROVE
ILLINOIS 60515

*To*
*Gilbert M. James*
*and*
*Charles W. Kingsley*
*who in very different ways*
*combine the evangelistic*
*and prophetic dimensions*
*of the*
*Kingdom of God*

# CONTENTS

# Preface

*This book is written out of frustration and hope. Frustration with so much that I have seen and experienced in the contemporary church which has led me to question seriously whether the church as we know it can ever be renewed. But also hope—hope because of the resurrection of Jesus Christ, and because of those faithful communities of believers down through history which have honestly followed the Risen One and have revealed the reality of the community of the King.*

*Though in some ways the present book is a sequel to* The Problem of Wineskins, *a book on church structure, the focus here is upon the relationship between the Church and the Kingdom of God. Only secondarily is the question of church structure examined. The book is essentially an expansion of a paper entitled "The Church As God's Agent of Evangelism" which was prepared for the 1974 International Congress on World Evangelization in Lausanne, Switzerland. Chapter nine comprises, in somewhat revised form, material which appeared as a chapter in* The New Face of Evangelicalism, *edited by C. René Padilla (InterVarsity Press, 1976).*

*In reading the New Testament I am impressed that early Christians and New Testament writers understood the Church as part of God's dramatic action in Jesus Christ of reconciling all things to himself, "things in heaven and on earth" (Eph. 1:10). The New Testament calls this reconciling work the Kingdom of God. This book* *probes the relationship between the Church and the Kingdom.**

I have tried in these pages to set forth what Scripture teaches and what history illustrates about the Church. I have taken the biblical record very seriously as God's authoritative and reliable revelation to us. But in speaking of the Church and the Kingdom I have been little concerned with following specific theories, theologies or traditional viewpoints. No particular millennial system is espoused or presupposed in the book. There is a dynamic character to the Church and the Kingdom which no millennial or dispensational theory (whether modern or medieval) can comprehend. Obviously, this book cannot totally comprehend it either.

I am especially indebted to a number of people who read the manuscript and offered valuable criticisms. I have taken these criticisms into account in making final revisions. Especially I would like to thank John F. Alexander, Donald W. Dayton, G. Roger Schoenhals, Ralph D. Winter and my father, Edmund C. Snyder, for their criticisms and suggestions, though perhaps none of them will agree totally with the final result.

---

*In this book the words Church and Kingdom are capitalized when they refer to the one true Church and Kingdom of God. When referring to specific local or historic expressions of the Church, or when used as adjectives, they are not capitalized.

## Introduction:
## Does the Church
## Bring the Kingdom?

Is it good news when the Church succeeds?

A theologian once wrote, "Speaking frankly, I do not really know whether the current prosperous condition of the church is more pleasing to God than its earlier humility. That earlier condition was perhaps better, but the present one is more agreeable!"[1]

Those were the words of Otto of Freising, apologist for the Holy Roman Empire in the twelfth century. Otto identified the Kingdom of God with the Church and saw the Kingdom coming to fruition in the political and ecclesiastical order of his day. Yet apparently he was attracted to the "weakness" and simplicity of the early church. The longing for a return to primitive Christianity eventually became a self-conscious impulse toward reform which led to what some have called "the renaissance of the twelfth century," and which reached its spiritual high point in Francis of Assisi and his humble band of followers.

The "success" of the Church at various points in history caused uneasiness which, joined with a new vision of its early days, prompted reassessment, reform, even renewal. The Protestant Reformation is the most well-known of several such times. Again in our day Jesus' followers might do well to ponder the contrast between the seeming prosperity of the present and the humility of the first-century Christian community.

Too little attention has been given to the doctrine of the Church in much modern thinking about evangelism, discipleship and social action. Donald Bloesch in *The Evangelical Renaissance* observes that "the doctrines of the church and the sacraments are conspicuously lacking in much contemporary evangelical writing."[2] Yet proper thinking about the Church's ministries can only occur in the context of a clear, biblical understanding of the Church itself. It is encouraging, then, that in new ways the question of the Church is now beginning to come to the fore in orthodox Protestantism. One sign of the Spirit's moving in very recent years has been a new concern to discover the biblical picture of the Church. There is a growing awareness that many problems of contemporary Christianity trace directly to the view of the Church as essentially static, organizational and institutional.

In this book the Church is seen as the community of God's people—a people called to serve him and called to live together in true Christian community as a witness to the character and values of his Kingdom. The Church is the agent of God's mission on earth.[3] But what is that mission? It is nothing other than bringing all things and, supremely, all people of the earth under the dominion and headship of Jesus Christ. If not all come willingly, nevertheless, every knee will bow and every tongue will confess that Jesus Christ is Lord (Phil. 2:10-11).

But to say the Church is the agent of God's mission on earth is equivalent to saying the Church is the agent of the Kingdom of God. The Church is the messianic community—the community of those who recognize the true Messiah, already confess him as Lord and proclaim his good news to the ends of the earth.

So *the Church is the agent of the Kingdom of God.* To speak of either the evangelistic or prophetic role of the Church without relating these to the Church's kingdom mission is to lose the biblical perspective and develop a truncated vision of the Church's calling. Biblically, neither evangelism nor social action make full sense divorced from the fact of the Christian community as the visible, earthly expression of the Kingdom of God.

The Church is the only divinely-appointed means for spreading the gospel.[4] As Melvin Hodges has written, "The Church is God's agent in the earth—the medium through which He expresses Himself to the world. God has no other redeeming agency in the earth."[5] The gospel call is a call *to something,* and that something is more than a doctrine or an experience or a heavenly juridical transaction or the exercise of faith or even, exclusively, Jesus Christ. The gospel intends to call persons *to the body of Christ,* that is, the community of believers with Jesus Christ as its essential and sovereign head.[6]

So the Church is God's agent for establishing his Kingdom. It is the primary means by which he is accomplishing his reconciling purpose. Therefore, the Church is inseparable from God's cosmic design to sum up all things in Jesus Christ (Eph. 1:10)—the essence and goal of the Kingdom.

I purposely speak of the Church as the *agent* of the Kingdom, rather than merely as a sign or symbol of the Kingdom or as an inanimate tool in God's hands. *Agent* comes from the Latin verb *agere,* "to act." It is an action word. God acts creatively and redemptively. His action involves "a plan for the fulness of time, to unite all things" in Jesus Christ. In this plan not only does God act, people also act. The Kingdom of God is the work of God; yet within God's plan there is room for human action. God's grace is that great. So the Church is never a lifeless tool in God's hands. It is not merely object but also subject. It does the work of God; yet this continues to be, literally, the work *of God.* So the Church in relation to the Kingdom is not an event, it is an act. More than a symbol, it is an agent.

Jesus came preaching the Kingdom. He went about "teaching in their synagogues, preaching the good news of the kingdom, and healing every disease and sickness among the people" (Mt. 4:23). His message, "Repent, for the kingdom of heaven is near" (Mt. 4:17), was the same message John had preached (Mt. 3:2), for the Kingdom had actually appeared in space and time in the very person of Jesus. Over eighty times in the Gospels Jesus refers to the Kingdom.[7] He even told stories about the Kingdom (Mt. 13) which give us an idea of how the Kingdom comes. Jesus' mission was to tell the good news of the Kingdom, show what the Kingdom was like, demonstrate its works, tell how to enter it, and establish the messianic community in embryonic form. He died on the cross and rose again to defeat the kingdom of evil and bring in the age of the Kingdom of God.

What did Jesus talk about after his resurrection? He appeared to his followers "over a period of forty days and spoke about the kingdom of God" (Acts 1:3). This was his subject matter. When the disciples wanted to know if now, finally, Jesus was going to "restore the kingdom to Israel," Jesus said the important thing was that they would be his witnesses, through the power of the Holy Spirit, to the ends of the earth (Acts 1:6-8). Their witness—the Church's witness—would have kingdom significance.

But we need to define the Kingdom of God somewhat more precisely. The Kingdom is the dominion or reign of God and not primarily a place or a realm. Biblically, the Kingdom "refers first to a reign, dominion, or rule and only secondarily to the realm over which a reign is exercised."[8] Therefore, to speak of the Kingdom of God is to remind ourselves that God is the sovereign Lord. "The earth is the LORD's and the fulness thereof" (Ps. 24:1).

The Old Testament does not speak of "the Kingdom of God" as such, but through the Psalms and the Prophets it continually reminds us that God is King.[9] In the New Testament the mystery of the Kingdom is that God's dominion and plan center in the person of Jesus Christ. He is the Messiah, the anointed Son of the King. He is God incarnate, "the Word made flesh." And Jesus came preaching the Kingdom, announcing that in him the rule, reign and dominion of God were present on earth in a new way.

Look at what Jesus said and did. He spoke of the Kingdom; he gathered the Church. He did not say much about the Church, and he refused to set up the kind of Kingdom people expected. Instead he spoke of the "mystery" of the Kingdom. Through his life, death, resurrection and visitation at Pentecost he established not the Kingdom but the Church, the community entrusted with living and proclaiming the mystery of the Kingdom to the ends of the earth.

Jesus speaks of the Kingdom of God; Paul speaks of God reconciling all things through Jesus Christ (2 Cor. 5:19; Col. 1:20). These are two ways of saying the same thing, for God is reigning and reconciling through Christ.

This understanding of the Kingdom of God may be clarified by looking at what the New Testament calls "the mystery" or "secret" (*mustērion*) of the Kingdom.[10] Jesus said to his disciples, "The secret of the kingdom of God has been given to you" (Mk. 4:11; see Mt. 13:11 and Lk. 8:10). Through faith in Jesus the disciples were able to understand what to others was hidden—that in the very person of Jesus Christ the Kingdom of God had drawn near. Later they would understand that all God's promises concerning his Kingdom would come to fulfillment through Jesus Christ.

Paul speaks of "the mystery of the gospel" (Eph. 6:19), "the mystery of Christ" (Col. 4:3), "the mystery of godliness" (1 Tim. 3:16). He saw this mystery as the unfolding of God's previously hidden purposes, now revealed in the events of Jesus' life, death and resurrection, and in the creation of a reconciled and reconciling community of believers through the proclamation of Christ (Rom. 16:25-26; 1 Cor. 2:7-10;

Col. 1:26-27; 1 Tim. 3:16). Paul speaks most fully of this "mystery" in Ephesians 3:2-10, where he says the "mystery of Christ" is that salvation is now extended to the Gentiles, as well as to the Jews. Now both Jew and Gentile are members of "one body," the Church. God's will is that "now, through the church, the manifold wisdom of God should be made known to the rulers and authorities in the heavenly realms, according to his eternal purpose which he accomplished in Christ Jesus our Lord" (Eph. 3:10). Or again, "the mystery of his will" is "to bring all things in heaven and on earth together under one head, even Christ" (Eph. 1:9-10).

Jesus speaks of "the mystery of the kingdom"; Paul speaks of "the mystery of Christ." For Christ is the key to the Kingdom. The Kingdom of God is the ongoing reconciling work of God in Christ seen from the perspective of the final definitive establishment of God's dominion when Christ returns to earth. Christ must return to fully establish his Kingdom. But by his Spirit he now works on earth through his body, the Church.

Why is this a secret, a mystery? Scripture calls God's kingdom design a mystery for several reasons. It was hidden until Jesus Christ came. It was revealed by the Holy Spirit, not by human understanding. It is contrary to the wisdom of the world. It is present now in suffering and weakness. It is based solely on the work of Christ. It requires faith. And it will not be fully revealed until Jesus Christ returns to earth.

What then is the Kingdom of God? It is Jesus Christ and, through the Church, the uniting of all things in him. For the present it is the growth in the world of the grace, joy, health, peace and love seen in Jesus. The Kingdom is both present and future, both earthly and heavenly, both hidden and becoming manifest. It is as concrete and this-worldly as the dust on Jesus' feet or the Galilean wind in his hair; it is as costly as the crucifixion; it is as heavenly as the risen Christ sitting at the right hand of the Father. "It is expanding in society like the grain of mustard seed . . .; working toward the pervasion of society like the leaven in the lump."[11] Its truths and values are those taught and lived by Jesus Christ and delivered to the body of his followers. But this Kingdom can become fully manifest only when Jesus Christ returns to earth.

How should the Church and the Kingdom be perceived in these days between Jesus' first and second comings? We will now examine this question in the light of contemporary perceptions of the Kingdom and of the Church.

# 𝔬𝔫𝔢

## PERCEIVING
## THE KINGDOM

THE KINGDOM OF GOD DOES NOT COME VISIBLY,
NOR WILL PEOPLE SAY, "HERE IT IS,"
OR "THERE IT IS,"
BECAUSE THE KINGDOM OF GOD IS WITHIN YOU.
(LK. 17:20-21)

# 1

# KINGDOM
# CONSCIOUSNESS

Despite denominational and other differences, Christian churches within a given society often reveal a strikingly similar theological perspective. Denominational traditions may differ, but a common stance is frequently evident.

Such a common perspective exists within conservative American Protestantism today. Although it includes a wide variety of specific denominations and traditions, evangelicalism clearly exhibits a particular theological point of view, one marked by the shape of American culture and evangelicalism's common heritage in the modernist-fundamentalist controversy.

The 1960s saw the reaffirmation of evangelical Protestantism's social conscience. American Christianity's prefundamentalist social concern of the previous century was rediscovered, and books such as Timothy Smith's *Revivalism and Social Reform* became popular.

Few evangelicals will doubt that this development was good. If there indeed has been an "Evangelical Renaissance" (to use Donald Bloesch's phrase), this has meant, in part, the recovery of the gospel's social dimension and the end of the modernist-fundamentalist controversy that reigned from (roughly) 1900 to 1950.

But how far has evangelicalism come and where is it going?

Is it enough merely to reaffirm in word and act an evangelical social conscience? Does current evangelical theology rest on a sufficiently secure biblical basis to thrust creatively and faithfully into the future? And if it is true that evangelicalism is "slowly succumbing to an identity-crisis," as Carl F. H. Henry suggests,[1] what will this mean for evangelical social witness?

Even if evangelicalism has made significant progress in the past twenty-five years—theologically, institutionally and numerically—still the present theological basis is too narrow. Unless a more comprehensive and more penetrating vision of biblical truth is reached, there is danger that the "Evangelical Renaissance" may either degenerate into a new evangelical establishment or fragment into mutually exclusive pieces. Evangelicals must move beyond social conscience to a biblical kingdom consciousness.

**From Fundamentalism to Evangelicalism**    A quick historical review will clarify this point. Looking at the history of American Protestantism in this century, one can trace three more or less distinct stages:

1. *Uneasy Conscience.* This stage can for convenience be linked with the publication of Carl F. H. Henry's book *The Uneasy Conscience of Modern Fundamentalism* in 1947. In that book Henry wrote:

*The "uneasy conscience"... is not one troubled about the great Biblical verities, ... but rather one distressed by the frequent failure to apply them effectively to crucial problems confronting the modern mind. It is an application of, not a revolt against, fundamentals of the faith, for which I plead.*[2]

This stage came as the battlefield dusts were settling—both literally (World War 2) and figuratively (the modernist-fundamentalist controversy)—and theological conservatives had time for second thoughts. The possibility of self-criticism arose in at least some fundamentalist circles. Men such as Carl F. H. Henry and Harold Ockenga were in the forefront of the conscience probers.

The uneasy conscience stage ran from about 1947 until the early 1960s. The pricks of conscience over fundamentalism's one-sidedness provoked, or at least accompanied, several significant developments in the forties and fifties: the founding of Fuller Theological Seminary (1947), World Vision (1947) and the Evangelical Theological Society (1949), and the birth of *Christianity Today* (1956). The appearance of the National Association of Evangelicals somewhat earlier (1942) was not unrelated. Of parallel significance was the unmistakable impact of Billy Graham's mass evangelism from 1949 on. These developments have been chronicled adequately in Ronald Nash's *The New Evangelicalism*, Millard Erickson's *The New Evangelical Theology* and, more recently, in David O. Moberg's *The Great Reversal* and in *The Evangelicals* by Wells and Woodbridge.[3]

The result of fundamentalism's uneasy conscience was the birth of evangelicalism. This transition resulted in a new concern with social ethics and social involvement, a renewed emphasis on scholarship, and the emergence of a broader-based and more cordial apologetics. It led directly to the next step away from fundamentalism.

2. *Social Conscience.* No phrase has been used more widely in recent years to emphasize evangelicalism's broadened emphasis than *social conscience.* Typical is Sherwood Wirt's *The Social Conscience of the Evangelical,* published in 1968. This phase began in the mid-sixties and has continued to the present.

The marks of evangelicalism's awakened social conscience can be seen in the increased emphasis on social issues in the NAE and similar organizations, the mixing of social ministries into Billy Graham and Leighton Ford crusades, and greater evangelical sensitivity to the racial issue and the urban crisis with accompanying changes in evangelical college and seminary curricula and programs. The social conscience phase is most evident, however, in recent evangelical publishing. Examples are the numerous books dealing in one way or another with social questions, a greater emphasis on social issues in evangelical publications and the growing influence of "young evangelical" publications which major on social questions—notably *The Other Side* and *Sojourners*.[4] David Moberg chronicles a growing list of examples of "evangelism plus social action" in his book *The Great Reversal*. He concludes that today "evangelicals are awakening to their inconsistencies and returning to the totality of the Christian Gospel."[5]

American evangelicalism is probably now at the peak of the social conscience phase. Not only are there abundant calls for social concern and actual significant demonstrations of such concern, but a broad-based theological consensus for this has emerged.

In a word, this evangelical consensus says that evangelism and social concern go together and are both essential to the one gospel. Some examples reinforce the uniformity of this consensus. Sherwood Wirt writes, "To pit social action against evangelism is to raise a phony issue, one that Jesus would have spiked in a sentence. He commanded his disciples to spread the Good News, and to let their social concern be made manifest through the changed lives of persons of ultimate worth."[6] Carl Henry says, "The Biblical view declares both individual conversion and social justice to be alike indispensable. The Bible calls for personal holiness and for sweeping societal changes; it refuses to substitute private religion for social responsibility or social engagement for personal commitment to God."[7] Similarly, Leighton Ford comments, "It is a scandal when we as Christ's disciples compartmentalize our lives, putting our personal piety in one segment and our social responsibility in another"; the two go together.[8] Similar statements have been made by Billy Graham, Elton Trueblood, John Warwick Montgomery and many others.

The emergence of an evangelical social conscience was, to

many, a positive and welcome development. Perhaps it marked the end of the modernist-fundamentalist detour. If evangelicals have not yet had the social impact they should have, at least the failure has been diagnosed and a more biblical course charted.

But is the social conscience consensus really sufficient? Is it broad enough? I suggest that, timely as it is, this consensus still bears marks of the dichotomist thinking of the past. We need to go beyond this dichotomy to a more comprehensive vision. There are in fact signs that evangelicalism is moving toward a third stage.

If the social conscience consensus were boiled down to a formula, it might be this: God saves people who in turn have responsibility for evangelism and social action. The perspective is that of the individual Christian looking out upon the world. But there is another possible view, the perspective of one who steps back behind the evangelism/social action debate and attempts to view God's total plan for his creation. This is what Paul does in the first three chapters of Ephesians, when he speaks of God's plan to unite all things in Jesus Christ through the Church (Eph. 1:10; 1:20-23; 3:10). Here one sees not two poles—evangelism and social action—but one cosmic design. At the very center of this design is personal reconciliation to God through Christ, but within the circle one perceives a cosmic plan for the reconciliation of all things. If there were a formula, perhaps it would be: God in Christ is reconciling the whole creation to himself, and his action through the Church is central to his plan.[9]

Here and there signs that evangelicalism is now moving toward such a comprehensive vision appear.[10] This is the next stage.

3. *Kingdom Consciousness.* All salvation comes from God. All genuine renewal and reconciliation—whether personal, communal or cultural—trace back to God's action and, therefore, to his purpose and plan. Beginning with this awareness, one

can find the proper biblical place for every legitimate Christian emphasis, whether evangelism, social action, church renewal or discipleship.

The Scriptures emphasize the eternal purpose or plan or will of God, that which he is doing in history to bring about the reconciliation of all things. This divine purpose is identified with the Kingdom or reign of God.

The question is not one of adding a social dimension to an evangelistic gospel. Rather evangelism, conversion, social justice and other gospel emphases must be seen as part of God's cosmic/historical redemptive plan. This is contemporary Christian witness viewed in the light of the coming Kingdom.

To some extent Carl Henry already points in this direction in the last chapter of *A Plea for Evangelical Demonstration.* Henry writes, "The Bible envisages nothing less than a new man, a new society, a veritable new heaven and earth in which universal righteousness prevails."[11] Henry speaks of "the divine culture-mandate" given to humanity, and says that "both in perspective and practice, the Christian is to bear witness to the divine spiritual and moral dimension in work and leisure, in learning and the arts, in family and public life."[12] Here is the beginning of a perspective beyond social conscience: even now, before the return of Christ, Christians have responsibility for all of culture.

Francis Schaeffer represents another step in the direction of kingdom consciousness. Practically unheard of outside a small circle before the publication of *The God Who Is There* in 1968, Schaeffer is today perhaps the most widely-read evangelical theological writer. Why this popularity? One reason is certainly the inclusiveness of Schaeffer's analysis, that is, his insistence that all of culture is interrelated, that God's plan encompasses all areas of life, that no discipline or category is independent of biblical truth and values.

In *Pollution and the Death of Man* Schaeffer emphasizes, "As

Christ's death redeems men, including their bodies, from the consequences of the Fall, so His death will redeem all nature from its evil consequences."[13] Although this cosmic redemption will occur in fullness only "at the time when we are raised from the dead, we should be looking now, on the basis of the work of Christ, for substantial healing in every area affected by the Fall."[14]

Schaeffer cites the fourfold alienation that results from the Fall (from God, from ourselves, from other persons and from nature), and stresses that God is bringing about a partial restoration in each of these areas. "Christians ... are not simply called to say that 'one day' there will be healing, but that by God's grace substantially, upon the basis of the work of Christ, substantial healing can be a reality here and now."[15]

Schaeffer sounds a note here that goes beyond what most evangelicals—even those emphasizing social conscience—have been saying. Here is a global, cosmic perspective that sees God's plan in its space-time totality and focuses on what God is doing through the Church here and now. This represents a move, at least, in the direction of a new consciousness of the Kingdom of God.

**A Kingdom Consciousness Today**   Christians today need such a kingdom vision. Only theological clarity and breadth will withstand the stainless-steel technotopia of the secularist and the nebulous pseudotopia of the psychedelic.

A consciousness of the present reality of the Kingdom of God and confidence in it have certainly not been foreign to American Protestantism; rather they have been typical. H. Richard Niebuhr notes in *The Kingdom of God in America* that "the Great Awakening and the revivals were ushered in by a new awareness of the coming kingdom."[16] Niebuhr goes on to say,

*The expectation of the coming kingdom ... became the dominant idea*

*in American Christianity. If the seventeenth was the century of the sovereignty and the eighteenth the time of the kingdom of Christ, the nineteenth may be called the period of the coming kingdom. ... Among the Christians of America, at least, the optimism of the nineteenth century was intimately connected with the experience of the anticipated Christian revolution.*[17]

While the contemporary Christian may disagree with certain emphases of this earlier American kingdom consciousness, still it is significant that such a consciousness existed. It emphasized God's transformation of every sector of society, from the Church to art and science and government. What happened after 1890 or so was that social gospelers secularized this kingdom vision and conservatives spiritualized it. A polarization set in and the biblical balance was lost. The result was the modernist-fundamentalist controversy. Niebuhr argues that although "many interpreters of the so-called 'social gospel' have assumed that prior to 1907 or 1890 the hope of a kingdom on earth was practically nonexistent while Christians directed all their expectations to the heavenly city," this is in fact a caricature.[18] Mid-nineteenth-century evangelicals had an active kingdom consciousness that bore fruit in widespread social and cultural reform, as well as active evangelism. Donald W. Dayton has recently documented this evangelical revival-plus-reform movement in *Discovering an Evangelical Heritage.*[19]

From the perspective of today this nineteenth-century kingdom emphasis seems marred by an unbiblical optimism. Fundamentalism, of course, veered into an essentially pessimistic attitude, adopting premillennialism and a rigid dispensationalism. All optimism was reserved for the millennial kingdom, which could only come cataclysmically and only as temporal-historical conditions worsened: "the worse things get, the better it is."

Contemporary evangelicalism tends toward a more biblical balance between optimism and pessimism, but is weak in kingdom consciousness. Yet it is precisely a profound awareness of the dual nature of the Kingdom as both present and coming which is necessary to maintain such an equilibrium. Evangelicalism today needs a kingdom consciousness—an awareness of the Kingdom of God—similar to that of earlier American Protestantism, but one which is more biblically based.

What elements are essential for an evangelical kingdom consciousness today? Five ingredients are particularly crucial.

First, *an emphasis on the cosmic dimension of the gospel.* Personal salvation is the *center* of God's cosmic plan, but it is not the *circumference* of the plan. The whole first chapter of Ephesians teaches that personal redemption fits into an overall divine cosmic design, namely, the reconciliation of all things in Christ.[20] The entire Bible, in fact, speaks of God's cosmic design much more than is reflected in evangelical theology today.[21] This cosmic dimension needs to be rediscovered and explored. In traditional theological terms, we must recall that God is sovereign, and that Jesus Christ has conquered the principalities and powers.

Second, *a recovery of the dynamic breadth of the Word of God.* It is an oversimplification to say that neo-orthodoxy saw Christ as the Word of God while evangelicalism sees the Bible as the Word of God. Still, there is truth in this statement. But it is clear from the Bible itself that "the word of God" is a dynamic reality—God communicating—which embraces both Jesus Christ and the Bible. Evangelicals need to be wise enough to continue to affirm that the Bible is the infallible Word of God, while going on to say that the Word is much more than a book. It is dynamic, creative, ever new. It is, in fact, "living and active, sharper than any double-edged sword" (Heb. 4:12). The context shows clearly that this passage does not refer only to the Bible.

Third, *a recovery of a sense of history.* The Kingdom of God is a historical fact. It does not burst full-blown upon the world scene unrelated to history, but is in some sense the result of God's action throughout history, and supremely in the events of Christ's life, death and resurrection. It is true that the definitive establishing of the Kingdom awaits the return of Christ; it is also true that God is now working in history, principally "through the church" (Eph. 3:10). Evangelicals need to reaffirm the significance of human action within the historical process while neither dichotomizing nor deifying history.

Fourth, *a new emphasis on the ethics of the Kingdom.* Jesus' teachings make plain that the Kingdom of God in its present reality means a lifestyle of discipleship. "The church is the suffering form of the kingdom of God."[22] The present expression of the Kingdom demands crucifixion ethics not triumphal ethics. The Church today must not live as if the Kingdom were already fully established; it is called to live the paradox of the King who ended up on a cross. Therefore, a new consciousness of the Kingdom today means a new awareness of the demands of discipleship.

And finally, *a Christian view of culture* is a necessary component of a kingdom vision. There is a cultural mandate for the Christian as well as an evangelistic mandate. The gospel concerns itself with all of society, not merely with the institutional church. And God's sphere of action is not limited to the circle of believers but encompasses all of creation, as the Bible repeatedly reminds us.

Evangelicals rightly insist on the centrality and priority of personal conversion and of the edification of the Christian community, the Church. They often recognize, as well, that conversion and Christian community imply a fundamental social responsibility. But this vision must go further. It must take in the whole question of culture and culture formation. What are the implications of the biblical view of reality for art, education, politics, music, philosophy? All these areas affect persons; all are projections of human work and human perception of reality. And all must come under the lordship of Christ.

The Kingdom of God has not fully come but it is coming. Its full establishment awaits the return of Christ. But through the life and work of God's people—the Church—it continues to expand and grow. And understanding the Kingdom is closely bound up with understanding the Church.

# 2

## MODELS
## OF THE CHURCH

Where you stand makes a difference in what you see. And where you stand with respect to the Church, accordingly, affects how you think the gospel should be lived out and what you think the Kingdom of God really means.

How should we look at the Church? What are the basic figures and metaphors by which we may understand it? To ask these questions is to identify a certain shift today in Christianity's self-understanding.

Some thirty-five hundred evangelical leaders concerned with missions and evangelism in all parts of the world met in Lausanne, Switzerland at the 1974 International Congress on World Evangelization. The Congress issued a notable document, the Lausanne Covenant, expressing the consensus of the participants on a number of issues relating to world evangelization. Of particular interest for this book is what is said about the Church.

Lausanne was certainly no formal ecclesiastical assembly or "ecumenical council" in the technical sense. Yet in one sense the International Congress on World Evangelization does stand in line with the historic councils of the Church. Considering the total number of participants and the breadth of denominational and geographic representation (even though

this representation was unofficial and was theologically restricted), one could argue that in some ways Lausanne has
more right to the title *ecumenical* than many of the "ecumenical councils" of history. And despite the fact that the Congress self-consciously did not see itself as an ecclesiastical
council, it would be naive to read its significance as having no
relationship to the conciliar history of Christianity. This is
especially so if it is indeed true, as the Covenant affirms, that
the Church is "the community of God's people rather than an
institution."

The Lausanne Covenant is therefore significant as the expression of an incipient worldwide consensus, among evangelicals at least, as to the nature of the Church. For that reason what it says about the Church deserves closer scrutiny.

The two key statements on the Church in the Lausanne
Covenant occur in Section 6, "The Church and Evangelism":
"The church is at the very center of God's cosmic purpose and
is his appointed means of spreading the Gospel. . . . The
church is the community of God's people rather than an institution, and must not be identified with any particular culture, social or political system, or human ideology." Elsewhere
the Covenant speaks of God's calling "a people to himself"
(Section 1) and of the "new community" summoned by Christ
(Section 4).[1] It is clear that Lausanne saw the Church chiefly in
terms of *community* and *peoplehood*. The document entitled
"A Response to Lausanne," coming out of the impromptu
"radical discipleship" caucus held during the Lausanne
conference, likewise pointed to "community," speaking
of the Church as a "charismatic" and "messianic" community.[2]

The significance of these statements lies as much in what
they do not say as in what they do. Their importance becomes
more obvious when they are placed alongside both traditional
Protestant formulations of the Church and the declarations of
Vatican II.

**The Reformation View**   The view of the Church espoused by the Protestant Reformers was given classic expression by Luther and Melanchthon in the Confession of Augsburg (1530): the Church is "the congregation of the saints, in which the Gospel is rightly taught and the sacraments rightly administered." Its "true unity" is based upon "unity of belief concerning the teaching of the Gospel and the administration of the sacraments."[3] Here the Church is seen fundamentally in terms of right belief, right teaching and right order. This definition of the Church, as E. Gordon Rupp has observed, "tended to influence all later definitions."[4]

More Calvinistic in tone is the Westminster Confession, a century later, which said the Church, invisibly, is "the whole number of the elect" and, visibly, "all those throughout the world that profess the true religion, together with their children."[5] The emphasis here is on election, right belief and, implicitly, on the sacraments and right order.

Although these statements are quite different, three things stand out: (1) primary emphasis is put on the gospel rather than on obedience to the hierarchy; (2) incorporation into the Church is seen as principally a matter of right belief or profession; and (3) the figures of community, peoplehood or body are not primary. The emphasis is shifted from the institution of the Roman Catholic ecclesiastical system to the institution of the proclaimed Word and the administered sacraments.

In the sixteenth century it was difficult to conceive of the Church as a people distinct from the rest of society or as a specific community separate from the world. Such a conception of the Church was so revolutionary as to be heretical and so threatening as to appear politically subversive. Largely for this reason, those who did go so far as to affirm the right and necessity of the Church to be a separate, distinct community of God's people—the Anabaptists—died by the hundreds for their faith. It is certainly more than coincidence that the contemporary rediscovery of Anabaptism has paralleled a new emphasis on the Church as community and as a people.[6]

**A Mixture of Metaphors**  The basic models or metaphors by which one understands the Church are more potent than they may at first appear. The Jesuit theologian, Avery Dulles, has pointed this out in his book, *Models of the Church.*[7] Dulles shows that though there are many valid figures for the Church, different figures or models have prevailed at different times. Today several models are current, and views concerning specific aspects of the Church are determined to a great extent by the particular model presupposed.

Peter Savage suggests that four models of the Church are especially common today. Many see the Church as a *lecture hall* where believers go to hear the Bible expounded. For others the Church is a *theater* where the faithful assemble to witness the drama of the sacrament enacted before them. Again, the Church may be seen as a *corporation*, efficient and highly program-oriented with a full-time pastoral team involved in retailing religion to the masses. Finally, Savage suggests that many see the Church as a *social club* which some people join to have certain needs met, just as one might join any other organization to have other needs met. Savage then goes on to discuss the Church as the eschatological and sacramental community of disciples.[8]

Dulles himself discusses five basic models which have operated throughout history: The Church as *institution*, as *mystical communion*, as *sacrament*, as *herald* and as *servant*. These metaphors are not mutually exclusive nor does any one encompass the whole truth about the Church—which after all remains a mystery. I believe Dulles is correct, however, in saying that "although all the models have their merits, they are not of equal worth, and some presentations of some models must positively be rejected."[9]

My interest is especially in the first two of Dulles's models—

the Church as institution and as mystical communion—because a certain polarity is found here and the question of the priority of one model over another, in the light of Scripture, comes most sharply into focus.

Historically, Roman Catholic theology has so stressed the institutional nature of the Church as the "perfect society" that the Church as institution may be said to have been the primary model behind Roman Catholic ecclesiology, at least from the Counter Reformation until recent years. But as Dulles points out, Vatican II marked a shift in emphasis. Cardinal Joseph Suenens gives graphic expression to this shift in his book, *A New Pentecost?* He testifies,

*When I was young, the Church was presented to us as a hierarchical society: it was described as "juridically perfect," having within itself all the powers necessary to insure and promote its own existence. This view reflected an image of the Church which was closely modeled on civil, even military society: there was a descending hierarchy, a uniformity which was considered as an ideal, and a tight discipline which extended to the smallest detail. . . .*[10]

Suenens points out, however, that "at the same time . . . another vision of the Church was gradually taking shape before our eyes." A number of Catholic theologians began to speak of the Church as the mystical body of Christ, and this paved the way for the statements of Vatican II. Says Suenens,

*The Second Vatican Council emphasized the Church as the People of God on pilgrimage, at the service of the world. . . . This was to stress the priority of baptism and the radical equality of the children of God, and automatically implies a reform of the concept of the Church which we today call "pyramidal," thus situating ministry within the heart and at the service of the whole ecclesiastical body. The perspective became more evangelical and less juridical without however repudiating the role of the hierarchy.*[11]

This statement, coming from so eminent a Catholic spokesman, is significant at several levels. From the standpoint of this chapter, its primary importance is its documentation of a major Roman Catholic shift in emphasis from the Church as institution to the Church as community and people. The same point is made by Dulles:

*Vatican Council II in its Constitution on the Church made ample use of the models of the body of Christ and the Sacrament, but its dominant model was rather that of the People of God. This paradigm focused attention on the Church as a network of inter-personal relationships, on the Church as community. This is still the dominant model for many Roman Catholics who consider themselves progressives and invoke the teaching of Vatican II as their authority.* [12]

It would be easy to exaggerate the significance of this shift from an institutional toward an organic/communal view of the Church. One must remember that the institutional character of the Church and the prerogatives of the hierarchy were explicitly reaffirmed by Vatican II. Yet a certain downgrading of the institutional concept in favor of one based on the symbols of peoplehood and community is obvious.

**The Models of Lausanne** Interestingly, both the Lausanne Covenant and the documents of Vatican II emphasize the same basic concept of the Church: the Church is the community of God's people. [13] As already noted, this signals a major shift in emphasis in Roman Catholic theology—a change which will likely work as yeast throughout the Catholic world.

The Lausanne Covenant, however, marks a similar major shift in understanding the Church on the part of evangelical Protestantism. [14] The shift may not be as great since Protestantism was never totally wedded to the hierarchical view of the Church. But that the Lausanne Covenant does represent a major change in models for the Church's self-understanding is obvious to anyone who compares its statement on "The Church and Evangelism" with such historic Protestant affirmations on the Church as the confessions of Augsburg and Westminster. It may therefore signal both a new evangelical concern with ecclesiology and a shift toward a less institutionalized view of the Church.[15]

If the Reformers did not specifically endorse the institutional/hierarchical view of the Church, neither did they have reason to reject it. William R. Estep perhaps goes too far in stating that "the Reformation was a revolt against papal authority but not against the Roman concept of the church as an institution,"[16] for in reducing the sacraments to two the Reformers shattered much of the medieval Roman Catholic ecclesiastical system. Even so, the Augsburg Confession is certainly compatible with an institutional understanding of the Church, if in fact it does not actually presuppose it.

Mainstream Protestantism thus has inherited concepts which lend themselves to an institutional understanding of the Church. This is most clear in the almost universal Protestant acceptance of the clergy-laity distinction preserved by exclusive clerical ordination, and in the practice of calling denominational structures "churches."

Such tradition can easily combine with the secular trends of modern society to produce an essentially institutional/organizational view of the Church which clashes with the idea of the Church as community and as a people. The modern technological revolution with its technocracy tends to reinforce the concept of the church-as-institution. This produces a concept of the Church which is overly concerned with institutional and technical modes of operation and dangerously susceptible to management and behavioral techniques which owe more to B. F. Skinner than to Paul or Jesus.

Significantly, Jesus rejected both religious and political hierarchical models for his followers in two related passages, Matthew 20:20-28 and 23:1-12.[17] Here we find such radical statements as these: "You know that the rulers of the Gentiles lord it over them, and their high officials exercise authority over them. Not so with you. Instead, whoever wants to become great among you must be your servant, and whoever wants to be first must be your slave" (Mt. 20:25-27). "You are not to be called 'Rabbi,' for you have only one Master and you are all brothers. . . . Nor are you to be called 'teacher,' for you have one Teacher, the Christ" (Mt. 23:8, 10). Hierarchical arrogance and titles which create distinctions among believers are called into question. Christ's followers are seen as brothers and fellow servants.

In describing the Church as "the community of God's people rather than an institution," Lausanne endorsed a view of the Church which is both radically biblical and practically important. The Lausanne Covenant does not, of course, give a full definition of the Church, nor did the Congress on World Evangelization intend to write a doctrinal statement as such. Since the word *institution* has such a wide range of meanings, the Covenant might preferably have said that the Church is not *primarily* an institution, rather than ruling out any institutional aspect whatsoever. But the statement as issued is a significant one and may be a step toward a more authentic, biblical understanding of the Church.

**The Church and the Kingdom**   As Dulles suggests, no one model can fully define the Church or what God is doing through it. A plurality of models and figures should be used to help us understand the Church's varied richness.

But some models logically must have priority over others. Biblically it would seem more valid to understand the Church as the community of God's people rather than as a hierarchical institution or a "juridically perfect society."[18] Certainly biblical figures such as the people and the flock of God, the body and bride of Christ, and the community or fellowship of the Holy Spirit have priority over other less specifically biblical models.

I am convinced that a properly biblical understanding of the Kingdom of God is possible only if the Church is understood—predominantly, if not exclusively—as a charismatic community and God's pilgrim people, his kingdom of priests. In this book I will attempt to show why this is the most valid way today to understand the Church.

Some may argue, of course, that this shift in models is only an accommodation to modern society. The idea of persons and people has been rediscovered and exploited by advertising and the media. Every bank, store and giant corporation wants to be known as "people who help people" or as "your kind of people" or as "people just like you." Isn't the Church merely tagging along with this trend?

Yes and no. What has been happening is this: the growth of interlocking, computerized, automated technology in education, government, marketing and industry has made the individual person feel less independent, less in control and more threatened by impersonal forces he neither understands nor knows how to deal with. The advertising media, not caught napping, have quickly discerned this trend and have embarked on a shrewd, computerized campaign to assure people there really is a human being behind each machine. U. S. Steel is not really a giant conglomerate; it's just a bunch of nice people trying to be helpful.

The Church can either exploit this trend and use it to manipulate people and their beliefs, or it can go deeper and ask the more fundamental questions: What is the Church, in truth? What is the biblical picture? Increasingly, modern society is like a bionic man: it looks soft, human, vulnerable and friendly on the outside, but underneath it's a mass of steel and wires, and no one is quite sure who is in control. The Church too can be merely smooth-running machinery with a veneer of personalism. Or it can be a radically biblical, caring community of believers totally sold out to Jesus Christ.

The latter, it seems to me, is what the Kingdom of God is all about. But it must be seen as God's people in relation to God's Kingdom or, in other words, as the messianic community, the community of the King.

# two

## UNDERSTANDING
## THE KINGDOM COMMUNITY

THIS IS WHAT THE KINGDOM OF GOD IS LIKE.
A MAN SCATTERS SEED ON THE GROUND.
NIGHT AND DAY, WHETHER HE SLEEPS
OR GETS UP, THE SEED SPROUTS AND GROWS,
THOUGH HE DOES NOT KNOW HOW.
ALL BY ITSELF THE SOIL PRODUCES GRAIN—
FIRST THE STALK, THEN THE HEAD,
THEN THE FULL KERNEL IN THE HEAD.
AS SOON AS THE GRAIN IS RIPE,
HE PUTS THE SICKLE TO IT,
BECAUSE THE HARVEST HAS COME.
(MK. 4:26-29)

# 3

## GOD'S
## MASTER PLAN

To be biblical we must see the Church and the gospel within the context of God's cosmic plan.

I believe that God is saving souls and preparing them for heaven, but I would never accept that as an adequate definition of the Church's mission. It is much too narrow. It is not a biblical definition, for the Bible speaks of a divine master plan for the whole creation.

**Master of a Great Household**  What is this cosmic plan? It is stated most concisely in the first three chapters of Ephesians, and it is here I will begin my biblical analysis. Two striking facts emerge from these chapters. First, God has a plan and purpose. Second, this plan extends to the whole cosmos.

Paul speaks of "the will of God" (1:1), "his pleasure and will" (1:5), "the mystery of his will according to his good pleasure, which he purposed in Christ" (1:9). Paul repeatedly says God "chose," "appointed" and "destined" us according to his will. Paul wished to speak of the Church as the result of, and within the context of, the plan and purpose of God.

Note especially Ephesians 1:10. The word sometimes translated "plan" is *oikonomia,* which comes from the word for "house" or "household." It refers to the oversight of a household, or to the plan or arrangement for household management. The idea "is that of a great household of which God is the Master and which has a certain system of management wisely ordered by Him."[1] Here is an orderly, premeditated divine plan or design for salvation.[2] Paul's figure of speech is particularly apt since he elsewhere refers to the Church as "God's household," *oikeios* (Eph. 2:19), and the same figure sometimes extends to the whole inhabited world. (*Ecumenical* comes from the same root.) Thus the idea of a cosmic plan is implicit in Paul's wording here. Paul may even have had in mind Jesus' parables of God as a householder who will settle accounts in the Kingdom of God (Mt. 13:27; 20:1, 11; 21:33; Lk. 13:25; 14:21).

Secondly, Paul sees God's plan in *cosmic perspective*. God's plan is "to unite all things in him, things in heaven and things on earth" (1:10 RSV). Five times Paul speaks of "the heavenly realms." God is the "Father of all, who is over all and through all and in all," and Christ has "ascended higher than all the heavens, in order to fill the whole universe" (4:6, 10). Particularly striking is 1:20-23, where Paul speaks of God's power *which he exerted in Christ when he raised him from the dead and seated him at his right hand in the heavenly realms, far above all rule and authority, power and dominion, and every title that can be given, not only in the present age but also in the one to come. And God placed all things under his feet and appointed him to be head over everything for the church, which is his body, the fullness of him who fills everything in every way.*

What a sublime starting point for understanding the Church and the Kingdom! We dare not hurry on to such favorite texts as Ephesians 2:8-9 or 4:11-12 or 6:10-20 without giving thorough attention to God's plan, hinging on Christ's victory. The Word of God is very clear: we begin to understand the Church and its mission as we see the Church as part of God's plan and purpose for the whole creation.

**Not Just "Plan B"**    But what is God's master plan? Simply this: *that God may glorify himself by uniting all things in Christ.* "God's plan is to unite and reconcile all things in Christ so that men can again serve their maker."[3]

The key idea is clearly that of reconciliation. God's plan is for the restoration of his creation, for overcoming, in glorious fulfillment, the damage done to persons and nature through the Fall. God's design for the reconciliation of all things in Christ reaffirms his original intention at creation now adjusted to the realities of the presence of sin in the world. But this is to speak humanly, from our underside view of reality; we must not suppose that God's cosmic plan for reconciliation is "Plan B," a second-best, back-up plan that God thought up because he failed at creation. For God's eternal plan predates both the Fall and the creation; it existed in the mind of God "before the creation of the world" (Eph. 1:4).[4]

This plan includes not only the reconciliation of people to God, but the reconciliation of "all things in heaven and on earth" (Eph. 1:10). Or, as Paul puts it in Colossians 1:20, it is God's intention through Christ "to reconcile to himself all things, whether things on earth or things in heaven, by making peace through his blood, shed on the cross." Central to this plan is the reconciliation of persons to God through the blood of Jesus Christ. But the reconciliation won by Christ reaches to all the alienations that resulted from our sin—within ourselves, between persons, between us and our physical environment. As mind-boggling as the thought is, Scripture teaches that this reconciliation even includes the redemption of the physical universe from the effects of sin as everything is brought under its proper headship in Jesus Christ (Rom. 8:19-21). Or as the New International Version suggests in translating Ephesians 1:10, God's purpose is "to bring all things in heaven and on earth together under one head, even Christ."[5]

This is God's master plan as seen in Ephesians. The same perspective comes through in Paul's other writings, especially in the first two chapters of Colossians. In 2 Corinthians 5:17-21 we learn that "God was reconciling the world to himself in Christ" and has entrusted to the Church both the message (*logos*) and the ministry (*diakonia*) of reconciliation. Of similar importance is the teaching of Romans 8 that the salvation freedom of the Christian will, in God's plan, extend to the whole of creation, for "the creation itself will be liberated from its bondage to decay and brought into the glorious freedom of the children of God" (Rom. 8:21).

In all these passages, Paul begins with the fact of individual and corporate personal salvation through Christ. From this he goes on to place personal salvation in cosmic perspective. We are permitted no either/or here, no spiritual tunnel vision. The redemption of persons is the *center* of God's plan, but it is not the *circumference* of that plan. Paul switches from a close-up shot to a long-distance view. He uses a zoom lens, for the most part taking a close-up of personal redemption, but periodically zooming to a long-distance, wide-angle view which takes in "all things"—things visible and invisible; things past, present and future; things in heaven and things on earth; all the principalities and powers—in the cosmic/historical scene. To understand truly what God in Christ has done for and through people, we must step back and look at God's entire cosmic design.

This is the Pauline view of God's master plan. Is it also the larger biblical view? In other Scriptures we find in essence the same perspective, for all Scripture is God-breathed. All the promises of cosmic restoration in the Old Testament apply here, reaching their climax in Isaiah's sublime vision (Is. 11: 6-9; 35:1-10; 65:17-25). The basic message of the book of Revelation is the harmonious uniting of all things under the lordship of Christ as all evil, all discord is destroyed. In a somewhat different context, this same "summing up" perspective is evident in Hebrews 1—2. Christ's parables of the Kingdom also point in this direction. And Isaiah, Peter and John speak of God creating a new heaven and a new earth (Is. 65:17; 66:22; 2 Pet. 3:13; Rev. 21:1). The testimony of Scripture is consistent: the same God who created the universe perfect, and sustains it in its fallen condition (Heb. 1:3), will restore all things through the work of Jesus Christ. As we shall see, it is Paul's particular task to emphasize the role of the Church in this cosmic redemption.

We cannot fully understand this cosmic design, this *oikonomia,* of God to unite all things in Christ. That is why Paul continually calls it a secret or hidden thing, a *musterion.*[6] But we can at least comprehend the basic outline of this plan and that this plan centers in Jesus' great reconciling, conquering work accomplished through his life, death and resurrection which is now being applied by the continuing work of the Holy Spirit.

**Now or Then?**   A very thorny problem here is the whole question of evil. If God is "reconciling all things to himself" through Jesus Christ, what is to become of those who reject Christ, and of Satan and his kingdom? Scripture does not answer all our questions here, but it does make plain that every alien authority and power will be destroyed (1 Cor. 15:24-25). Jesus himself spoke forcefully of the eternal destruction of the wicked (for instance, in Mt. 25:31-46). Revelation tells that Satan and his followers will suffer eternal judgment (20:10; 21:8) and that nothing impure will enter the New Jerusalem (21:27). These scriptures spell out what the Psalms repeatedly proclaim: God the King will conquer and destroy all his enemies. Our understanding of God's plan for reconciliation must be consistent with such scriptures, even if we cannot fully understand how this is possible.

When does God accomplish his reconciling work? Nearly all Christians admit that, in one sense or another, God is bringing history to a cosmic climax. But one branch of the Church has said, "Not now; *then!*" And in reaction, another group has said, "Not then; *now!*" The argument has centered on the nature of the Kingdom of God. Those who postpone any real presence of the Kingdom until after Christ's return ("Not now; *then!*") expect substantial renewal now only in the realm of individual religious experience, but not in politics, art, education or culture in general, and not even really, in the Church. On the other side are those who so emphasize present social renewal that both personal conversion and the space-time future return of Christ are denied or overshadowed, and our deep sinfulness and rebellion are not taken seriously.

Our hope should be that orthodox Christians throughout the world can come to see that the Kingdom of God is neither entirely present nor entirely future. There should be no false antithesis between the presence and the future coming of the Kingdom. The Kingdom of God (the uniting of all things under Christ) is now here, is coming and will come. This is certainly one of the lessons of the parables of the Kingdom.

Francis Schaeffer expresses this more balanced view when he speaks of a "substantial healing" now in all areas of alienation caused by sin. Avoiding the extremes sometimes found both in premillennialism and in postmillennialism, Schaeffer says Christians should not put all real reconciliation off into an eschatological future; neither should they expect total perfection now. What God promises is a substantial healing now and a total healing after Christ's return.[7]

What this means is that God has already begun the reconciliation of all things in human history. The "fullness of time" has come (Gal. 4:4; Eph. 1:10), but not in total fullness. The decisive act of God's reconciling work has taken place in Jesus Christ. God's cosmic plan is now unfolding.

The Church is not the Kingdom but it is bound up with the

Kingdom. It is the people of the Kingdom of God, the "eschatological community" which already lives under and proclaims God's rule.[8] Jesus' disciples are colaborers with him in revealing the Kingdom, for the head and body act together (2 Cor. 5:18—6:1; 1 Cor. 3:9). But even in its action the Church knows and confesses that the full coming of the Kingdom awaits Jesus' final revealing at his second coming.

We must now examine in more detail the question of the place of the Church in God's master plan.

# 4

## THE CHURCH
## IN GOD'S PLAN

What is the place of the Church in God's cosmic plan? What, in fact, is the Church?

A remarkable phrase occurs in Ephesians 3:10. God's cosmic plan, Paul says, is that "through the church, the manifold wisdom of God should be made known to the rulers and authorities in the heavenly realms."[1]

Let us look closely at this passage:

*In reading this, then, you will be able to understand my insight into the mystery of Christ, which was not made known to men in other generations as it has now been revealed by the Spirit to God's holy apostles and prophets. This mystery is that through the gospel the Gentiles are heirs together with Israel, members together of one body, and sharers together in the promise in Christ Jesus. . . . Although I am less than the least of all God's people, this grace was given to me: to preach to the Gentiles the unsearchable riches of Christ, and to make plain to everyone my administration [oikonomia] of this mystery, which for ages past was kept hidden in God, who created all things. His intent was that now, through the church, the manifold wisdom of God should be made known to the rulers and authorities in the heavenly realms, according to his eternal purpose which he accomplished in Christ Jesus our Lord. (Eph. 3:4-6, 8-11)*

The mystery, now made known, is that Gentiles as well as

Jews may share in God's promised redemption. In fact Jew and Gentile are brought together into "one body." Through Jesus Christ, as Paul had explained already, God has "made the two one and has destroyed the barrier, the dividing wall of hostility." So all Christians are one body, "one new man." This was "through the cross, by which he put to death their hostility" (Eph. 2:14-16).

Note the two dimensions here. Jewish and Gentile believers are reconciled both to God and to each other. They have joined in a reconciling relationship to Jesus that transcends and destroys their old hostility toward each other. No longer enemies, they are now brothers and sisters.

What then is the mystery of God's plan? It is that in Christ God acts with such redemptive power that he is able to overcome hatreds and heal hostilities. The mystery is not merely that the gospel is preached to Gentiles; it is that through this preaching Gentile believers are now "heirs together" and "members of one body."

It is in this context that we can understand verse 10. God's "manifold wisdom" is now made known through Christ's reconciling love which brings Jew and Gentile together as brothers in the community of God's people, the Church. But Jew and Gentile only? Was the miracle of the gospel exhausted by the reconciliation of Jew and Gentile in the first century A.D.? Certainly not! There is more to the mystery of God's plan. That initial, historic reconciliation shows us that God reconciles alienated persons and peoples to himself through the blood of the cross. It started with the reconciliation of Jew and Gentile and extends to free and slave, man and woman, black and white, rich and poor (Col. 3:10-11; Gal. 3:28).

This is why Paul can say that now "through the church, the manifold wisdom of God" is "made known to the rulers and authorities in the heavenly realms." For it is precisely in the Church where such reconciliation takes place. The Church is the fruit of Christ's reconciling love, and thus the revelation of God's manifold wisdom. And the Church, as Christ's body, shares Christ's reconciling work.

It is in this sense that the Church is the agent of God's plan. This is why Peter, Paul, James and John direct so many appeals to believers to be reconciled to each other, to watch carefully how they walk, to avoid all partiality, to walk in love and fellowship with the brothers and sisters. Their faithfulness, and ours, has kingdom significance.

The Church is more than God's agent of evangelism or social change; it is, in submission to Christ, the agent of God's entire cosmic purpose. The Kingdom of God is coming, and to the extent that this coming of the Kingdom occurs in history before the return of Christ, God's plan is to be accomplished through the Church. This agrees beautifully with what we have already seen: God's plan is to sum up all things in Christ, and the Church is the body of Christ. What God is doing in Jesus Christ and what he is doing in and through the Church are part of one whole.

However we understand the Church, it must be seen as related to God's kingdom purposes. But to say the Church is the agent of the Kingdom of God can mean radically different, and even contradictory, things according to how the Church itself is understood.[2] So we must look carefully at the biblical picture of the Church.

**The Biblical Perspective**   The Bible says the Church is nothing less than the body of Christ. It is the bride of Christ (Rev. 21:9), the flock of God (1 Pet. 5:2), the living temple of the Holy Spirit (Eph. 2:21-22). Virtually all biblical figures for the Church emphasize an essential, living, love relationship between Christ and the Church. This underscores the key role of the Church in God's plan and reminds us that "Christ loved the church and gave himself up for her" (Eph. 5:25). If the Church is the *body* of Christ—the means of the head's action in the world—then the Church is an indispensable part of the gospel, and ecclesiology is inseparable from soteriology. Therefore, to adopt what might be called an "anti-church stance" would be to dilute the very gospel itself and at the same time to demonstrate a misunderstanding of what the Bible means by "the church."

The Bible shows the Church in the midst of culture, struggling to be faithful but sometimes adulterated by unnatural alliances with paganism and Jewish legalism. In Scripture the earthly and heavenly sides of the Church fit together in one whole and do not leave us with two incompatible churches or with a split-level view of the Church. The Church is one; it is the one body of Christ that now exists both on earth and "in the heavenly realms" (Eph. 1:3; 2:6; 3:10). This view of the Church is sharply relevant for the modern age for reasons which are basic to the biblical view of the Church.[3]

First, *the Bible sees the Church in cosmic/historical perspective.* It is seen in the perspective of God's cosmic plan discussed in the previous chapter. The Church is the people of God which God has been forming and through which he has been acting down through history. In this sense the Church has roots that go back into the Old Testament, back even to the Fall. Its mission stretches forward into all remaining history and into eternity. This horizontal line is the historical dimension.

The cosmic dimension reminds us that our space-time world is really part of a larger, spiritual universe in which God reigns. The Church is the body given to Christ, the conquering Savior. God has chosen to place the Church with Christ at the very center of his plan to reconcile the world to himself (Eph. 1:20-23).

The Church's mission, therefore, is to glorify God by continuing in the world the works of the Kingdom which Jesus began (Mt. 5:16). This both justifies and demands the Church's broader ministry "to preach good news to the poor ... to proclaim freedom for the prisoners and recovery of sight for the blind, to release the oppressed, to proclaim the year of the Lord's favor" (Lk. 4:18-19).

Second, *the Bible sees the Church in charismatic, rather than in institutional, terms.* While the Church is, in a broad sense, an institution, it is more fundamentally a charismatic community. That is, it exists by the grace (*charis*) of God and is built up by the gifts of grace (*charismata*) bestowed by the Spirit. As seen biblically, it is not structured the same way a business corporation or university is, but is structured like the human body—on the basis of life. At its most basic level it is a community, not a hierarchy; an organism, not an organization (1 Cor. 12; Rom. 12:5-8; Eph. 4:1-16; Mt. 18:20; 1 Pet. 4:10-11).

Third, *the Bible sees the Church as the community of God's people.* Here the cosmic and the charismatic are united, and we see the Church as both within the world and as transcending the world.

Since the Church is the people of God, it includes all God's people in all times and in all places, as well as those who have now crossed the space-time boundary and live in the immediate presence of God. But the people of God must have a visible, local expression, and at the local level the Church is the community of the Holy Spirit. As Samuel Escobar has said, "God calls those who become his people to be part of a community. So the new humanity that Christ is creating becomes visible in communities that have a quality of life that reflects Christ's example."[4]

The Church finds its identity in this unified, complementary rhythm of being a people and a community, both within a city or culture and within the larger worldwide context. People and community together constitute what the New Testament means by *ekklesia,* the called-out and called-together Church of God.

The biblical figures of body of Christ, bride of Christ, household, temple or vineyard of God, and so forth, give us the basic idea of the Church. Any contemporary definition must be in harmony with these figures or models. But these are metaphors and not definitions. I believe the most biblical definition is to say the Church is *the community of God's people*. The two key elements here are the Church as a people, a new race or humanity, and the Church as a community or fellowship—the *koinonia* of the Holy Spirit.[5]

**The Community of God's People**    These twin concepts emphasize that the Church is, in the first place, people—not an institutional structure. They emphasize further that the Church is no mere collection of isolated individuals, but that it has a corporate or communal nature which is absolutely essential to its true being. And finally, these truths show that being a community and a people is a gift from God through the work of Jesus Christ and the indwelling of the Holy Spirit. It is not produced by human techniques or plans. The Church is constituted the people of God by the action of Jesus Christ, and this reality opens the door to the possibility of true and deep community. Here the figure of the body takes on added meaning, including both the fact of community and the fact of peoplehood (see Figure 1).

This concept of peoplehood is firmly rooted in the Old Testament and underlines the objective fact of God's acting throughout history to call and prepare "a chosen people, a royal priesthood, a holy nation, a people belonging to God" (1 Pet. 2:9; compare Ex. 19:5-6). The Greek word for "people" is *laos*, from which comes the English "laity." This reminds us that the *whole* Church is a laity, a people. Here the emphasis is on the *universality* of the Church—God's people scattered throughout the world in hundreds of specific denominations, movements and other structures. It is the inclusive, worldwide, corporate reality of the multitude of men and women who, throughout history, have been reconciled to God through Jesus Christ. This fact celebrates the moving of God in history to constitute a pilgrim people and is especially related to the concept of the covenant. *Seen in cosmic/historical perspective, the Church is the people of God.*

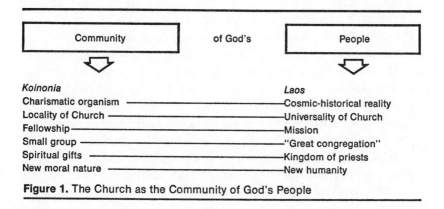

**Figure 1.** The Church as the Community of God's People

On the other hand, the Church is a community or fellowship, a *koinonia*. This emphasis is found more clearly in the New Testament and grows directly out of the experience of Pentecost. If peoplehood underlines the continuity of God's plan from Old to New Testament, community calls attention to the "new covenant," the "new wine," the "new thing" God did in the resurrection of Jesus Christ and the Spirit's baptism at Pentecost. The emphasis here is on the *locality* of the Church in its intense, interactive common life. *Seen as a charismatic organism, the Church is the community of the Holy Spirit.*

The Church as community emphasizes the local, temporal life of the Church in a given cultural context. Here we come down from the ethereal heights to the nitty-gritty business of Christians living together, sharing a common life. Here also we discover the basic fact that true community is essential for effective witness. And here too, as a result, we face the problem of wineskins—the necessity of dealing with practical structures in order to permit and encourage true community.

To speak of the Church as community is to take a somewhat more restricted view, since the Church is more than community. It is also the scattered people of God, the leaven of the gospel in the lump of the world, dispersed and working in every area of society. But community is essential, for where it is lacking, and where there are no working structures to nourish it, the leaven becomes inactive and the salt loses its savor.

It is critically important—especially in a worldwide, multicultural situation such as the Church faces today—to be clear that the essence of the Church is people, not organization; that it is a community, not an institution. The great divide in contemporary thinking about the Church is located precisely here. Biblically, the Church is the community of God's people, and this is a spiritual reality which is valid in every culture. But all ecclesiastical institutions—whether seminaries, denominational structures, mission boards, publishing houses or what have you—are not the Church. Rather, they are supportive institutions created to serve the Church in its life and mission. They are culturally bound and can be sociologically understood and evaluated. But they are not themselves the Church. And when such institutions are confused with the Church, or seen as part of its essence, all kinds of unfortunate misunderstandings result, and the Church is bound to a particular, present cultural expression.

One of the greatest needs of the institutional church today is to make a clear and sharp distinction between the church as biblically presented and the varied subsidiary ecclesiastical institutions—including denominational structures—which we so frequently confuse with the Church. Once this distinction is clearly understood, the Church will be freer to evangelize the world without unfortunate cross-cultural pollution. At the same time, all ecclesiastical organizations will have become desacralized and will be seen as structures which can be used, modified or discarded as need demands. The relationship between the Church, properly so-called, and institutional ecclesiastical structures will be discussed in some detail in chapter eight.

**The Steward of God's Grace**   The New Testament and the writings of the first church fathers show that the early church saw itself primarily as a charismatic community or as an organism, not as an institution or an organization. With the gradual institutionalization of the Church, however, the idea of the Church as organization became more prominent and largely crowded out the charismatic/organic view, especially in the West. Thus "in the history of theology the Church as assembled community of the faithful has been too often neglected in favour of the Church as institution," notes Hans Küng.[6]

In the biblical view God gives his gracious gift of salvation on the basis of Christ's work and through the agency of the Holy Spirit. This provides the basis of the Church's community life. The pure light of God's "manifold grace" (1 Pet. 4:10 NASB) is then refracted as it shines through the Church, as light through a prism, producing the varied, multicolored *charismata*, or gifts of the Spirit (see Figure 2). The Greek word *poikilos* ("manifold") in 1 Peter 4:10 and Ephesians 3:10 often expresses the idea of "many-colored," as in the variety of colors in flowers or clothing.[7] This suggests that the pure, intense but invisible light of God's glorious grace is made colorfully visible in the diversity of spiritual gifts in the Christian community.

This operation of the Holy Spirit provides the basis for the Church's diversity within unity (Eph. 4:1-12; 1 Cor. 12). The edification of the Church thus results from the exercise of spiritual gifts as "the whole body, joined and held together by every supporting ligament, grows and builds itself up in love, as each part does its work" (Eph. 4:16).

This is important for the Church's work and witness in the

world since the New Testament ties ministry to the exercise of spiritual gifts (Eph. 4:11-12). In order for the Church to be alive and growing, it must be based on a charismatic model,

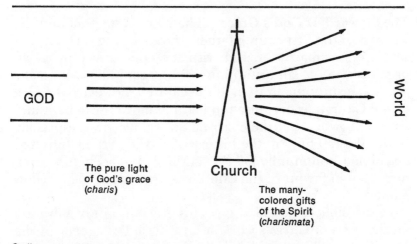

The pure light
of God's grace
(*charis*)

Church

The many-
colored gifts
of the Spirit
(*charismata*)

God's grace made visible to the world through the prism of the Church

**Figure 2.** The Church as "Steward of God's Many-Colored Grace" (1 Pet. 4:10-11)

not an institutional model. I make this contrast in order to call us back to what is most basic in the Church, to distinguish between the primary and secondary. This is an essential first step to a clear biblical understanding of the Church.

But, of course, to make this distinction raises many questions. Roman Catholic ecclesiology weds the charismatic and the institutional together, making the institutional primary and the charismatic secondary, subject to the authority of the institutional hierarchy. Since the institutional side of this view is clearly based on postapostolic tradition rather than on Scripture, I suggest that the traditional Roman Catholic solution to this problem is not a route Protestants can legitimately take. If our view of the Church is to rest squarely upon Scripture, we will have to insist on the priority of the charismatic over the institutional.[8]

It is necessary, however, to define more precisely what we mean by *institutional* and *charismatic,* since both words are understood in various ways. Let us consider first of all the question whether the Church may properly be called an institution.

**Is the Church an Institution?**   The Church as the people of God is definitely not an institution in the same sense that General Motors, Oxford University or the United Nations are institutions. This is true not because ecclesiastical institutions are empirically much different from secular institutions, for from a sociological standpoint the similarities are much more impressive than the differences. It is true rather because at its most basic and essential level the Church is something other than the institutional structures attached to it. One must not confuse the wineskins with the wine.

While the Church is not essentially an institution it does, however, have an institutional side in the same way the family does. And the Church has given rise to literally thousands of institutional structures which, sociologically, are close kin to other human organizations, corporations and bureaucracies.

It is sociologically naive to say the Church is in no sense an institution. Any pattern of collective behavior which has become habitual or customary is already an institution. In this broad sense the Lord's Supper is an institution; and even a small group Bible study, if it meets continually over a period of time, becomes an institution.

A certain degree of institutionalization is therefore inevitable and even desirable in the Church. It is simply one result of the fact that people live in space and time. Institutionalization would be unimaginable in eternity! Sociologist David O. Moberg has written, "Every religious organization has some degree of formalism or institutionalization. This is true even of groups that claim to be 'merely a fellowship, not a denomination,' and of those so informally and loosely organized that they claim to lack organization altogether."[9] And Moberg goes on to quote sociologists Douglass and Brunner:

*The attempt, then, to conceive of a non-institutionalized religion for modern man is sociologically infantile. It is an attack on rationality and ethical stability themselves. Religion cannot have currency without developing some generalized form, and generalized form implies habits resistant to change which are the essence of institutionalization.* [10]

In this sense some institutionalization of the Church is already evident in the New Testament—regular meetings in homes, some patterns of leadership, the celebration of the Lord's Supper, and apparently some prayers and confessions. The striking thing, however, is that these institutional elements were highly functional in the early church. No officially structured, formalized organizations in the sense of modern-day denominations or societies are to be found in the New Testament. Institutionalization of this more rigid, hierarchical and organizational type grew up only in the second and third centuries in part as a reaction to the charismatic excesses of the Montanists.[11]

These considerations suggest that the Church will inevitably manifest some institutional patterns, but no institution can ever be the Church. The Church can never be essentially an institution, even though it will necessarily be institutional in some aspects of its life.

Institutionalization is cumulative. And since the process inevitably is a mixture of the bad as well as the good, institutionalization will in time become deadening. Unless periodically reversed by institutional renewal, institutionalization will spell spiritual death for any church or movement. And since the gospel is life, it will at times lead to new movements seeking to restore the life of the primitive church when institutional structures become too rigid.[12]

In many areas the Church today is encased in rigid institutional structures which have impeded both growth and cultural relevance. Perhaps eighty per cent of such structures are not formal and official, but simply traditional and cultural. In North America, for instance, few if any denominations have adopted an article of faith stating that worship services must be held between ten and twelve o'clock Sunday morning, and yet this is one of the more rigid institutional patterns of North American Christianity. In many areas the same thing applies to liturgy, to the decision-making process, to ideas about the "clergy" and even to methods of evangelism. Much of this is simply tradition with no biblical roots. Only a small percentage is part of official church polity. Yet it is precisely this traditional, only half-perceived part of church structure which is most rigid, most resistant to change and often most deadening to the Church's life. I am reminded of John Wesley's initial reaction to "field preaching" in England, two centuries ago: "I should have thought the saving of souls a sin if it had not been done in church."

Is there hope for churches whose spiritual spontaneity and community life are stifled by rigid institutional forms? This is a question of institutional renewal. In such churches individual spiritual renewal among the believers is not enough, and by itself may provoke divisions and factions, just as new wine bursts old wineskins. A general principle for highly institutionalized churches is that *institutional renewal must accompany personal renewal.* Where this is not possible, or where the official guardians of the institution will not permit it, the old institution may have to be abandoned and new structures formed. There are times when old wineskins must be replaced by new ones. This has occurred repeatedly in church history.

Is the Church, then, an institution? In the broadest sociological sense it is. But even in this sense the institutional element is strictly secondary and derivative and must be functional. Nor does this affirmation imply that any and all institutional forms are legitimate for Church use. And in the more restricted sense of a formally constituted, hierarchical organization, the Church is not and never can be an institution, for the Church is the community of God's people. We must seek some other basis for understanding institutional, ecclesiastical structures and not confuse them with the essence of the Church.

**The Meaning of *Charismatic***   While some may object to the use of the word *charismatic* because of possible confusion with modern sociological or Pentecostal meanings of the word, I believe biblical accuracy calls us to reinstate the term if we wish to understand the Church today.[13]

I use *charismatic* here in the precise biblical sense of pertaining to the working and empowering of the grace or *charis* of God. The word reminds us both of that grace by which we are saved and of the special gifts of grace or charisms (*charismata*) which God promises to the Church. In this sense *charismatic* has no specific reference to glossolalia except in the general sense that tongues-speaking is one of the charisms mentioned in the New Testament.

The charismatic emphasis, and particularly the doctrine of spiritual gifts, is too important to be abandoned because of controversy over a word. *Charismatic* is a good and highly biblical term that needs to be restored to the Church in all its biblical significance. While the term is not the exclusive property of the charismatic movement, it does remind us that God has used this movement to call the larger body of Christ back to a neglected biblical emphasis. As Geoffrey Bromiley has commented, Reformation Protestantism today must come to "a fresh realization that Christian ministry is, and has to be, a charismatic movement."[14]

Those who feel the word *charismatic* has become too tainted or loaded to be useful today should consider such biblical terms as *presbyterian, episcopal, baptist* and *ecumenical.* All these words, like *charismatic,* come directly from New Testament Greek. Their modern, English connotations provide no good reason to abandon such words, but should rather motivate us to rediscover and reaffirm their true biblical significance for they say something significant about the Church.

As Bromiley suggests, the charismatic emphasis relates particularly to the ministry of the Church and, therefore, is important for the Church's role as agent of the Kingdom. Too often the churches I know are not charismatic communities in which each person ministers according to the gifts each has received. Rather they are little more than organizations not fundamentally different from other organizations in the same culture. Such institutionalized churches attempt vainly to minister through ever improved and expanding programs, training and techniques. Under unusually talented leadership such churches succeed, and everyone praises that success and uses it as a model. But in the majority of cases such spiritual technology fails, and only leaves local churches frustrated, starving for real spiritual fellowship, and wondering why someone else's sure-fire program "doesn't work" in their situation. For these reasons I suggest the contemporary church should self-consciously seek a charismatic model for its life to take the place of the prevailing institutional model.

A charismatic or organic model is one marked by community, interpersonal relationships, mutuality and interdependence. It is flexible and leaves room for a high degree of spontaneity. The Bible gives us such a model for the Church: the human body.

In contrast an institutional or organizational model is based on hierarchy, delegation of authority, impersonal relationships and formality. This is a legitimate form of human organization admirably suited to some kinds of endeavors, but it is not a proper model for Church structure. All biblical figures for the Church suggest a charismatic and organic, rather than an institutional, model: tree, vine, flock, family, nation, household and even the living and growing "holy temple." Legitimate institutional elements must be subordinate to the charismatic nature of the Church.

It would be appropriate at this point to begin a detailed discussion of church structure, showing the relevance of the charismatic/organic model for the structure of the community of God's people. We will postpone that discussion until chapter eight, however, in order to return to the basic question of this chapter and show more fully how the Church is the agent of the Kingdom of God.

**Leaven or Lifeboat?**   If the Church is essentially the community of God's people rather than an institution, then it is through the Church as people that God is accomplishing his cosmic plan—not, in the first place, through organizations and institutions, although these may be useful tools.

How, then, is God reconciling all things through Christ and through the Church? Does the Church accomplish God's cosmic purpose as a lifeboat for drowning souls? Is it primarily leaven to produce social ferment and change? Or is it like an ever-expanding dye that progressively penetrates all the structures of society, gradually turning the whole culture the color of righteousness? Or is the Church somehow a combination of all these?

The Ephesian letter reveals a twofold answer. The key passage is Ephesians 2:8-10:

*For it is by grace you have been saved, through faith—and this not from yourselves, it is the gift of God—not by works, so that no one can boast. For we are God's workmanship, created in Christ Jesus to do good works, which God prepared in advance for us to do.*

Two facts stand out here: first, all Christians have been saved by grace through faith, as the gift of God; and second, all Christians have been created to walk in God's foreordained good works. This means that the Church accomplishes God's plan by what it is (a redeemed community) and by what it does (good works). This is parallel to the life and work of Jesus Christ, the head of the Church, who was the Word of God made flesh and who said he came "to do the will of him who sent me and to finish his work" (Jn. 4:34).

So the Church's first task is truly to be the redeemed community. The genuine demonstration of Christian community is the first step toward accomplishing God's cosmic plan. This is miracle, and miracle attracts. God's plan calls for the Church to be a microcosm of that cosmic reconciliation which he is bringing. Thus, to the extent that the Church grows and expands throughout the world *and demonstrates true Christian community,* to that extent the Kingdom of God has come on earth!

The Church is not an inanimate tool in God's hand which he uses to accomplish his ends. This would violate the very concept of the Church which we have already outlined. The Church *is* before it *does.* "Christ loved the church and gave himself up for her" (Eph. 5:25). Therefore, the Church has value because it *is,* for it is the object of Christ's love. The love of Christ for the Church forbids any merely utilitarian view of the Church.

God does not use the Church as a lifeless object, for this would be contrary to all he wants to do within the Church. God's will is that the Church and each member within it attain "the full measure of perfection found in Christ" (Eph. 4:13). God wants spiritual growth-to-maturity in the Church. As the Church thus grows, it will accomplish God's plan to make known "through the church, the manifold wisdom of God . . . to the rulers and authorities in the heavenly realms" (Eph. 3: 10).

So the Church is not to be understood primarily as a means to the end of transforming society. This would be to trample over the uniqueness and infinite worth to God of the Christian community.[15] Besides, the amazing and profound fact is that the Church most transforms society when it is itself growing and being perfected in the love of Christ. In fact when the Church is taken merely as a means to transform society, very little is accomplished. For in that case the uniqueness of the Church is denied and we enter the battle on the same terms as secular and godless forces. We assume the battle for right and justice can be won by force, by technique, by doing. It can't. These very clearly are not the weapons of Christian warfare (Eph. 6:10-20).[16] Truly Christian transformation of culture comes through Christlike (and hence sacrificial) love, community and being.

But this fact by no means cancels out the responsibility to do, to act, to walk in the works of God. Rather, the being and the doing go together. The being is fundamental, but the doing is the natural result.

The thrust of Ephesians 2:10 is that we are saved by God in order that we may do good works. Part of God's purpose in saving us is that good works should be done. Further, these very works "God prepared in advance." This, not in the sense of predetermination of our acts, but in the sense of a pre-existing divine plan which God is bringing to realization through the saving of persons and through the works they consequently do.

So here again we encounter the fact of God's plan, his purpose. We are saved, not only for our own sake, but because there are specific things—particular works—which God, in his wisdom, wishes to accomplish. And he wishes to accomplish these through the activity of those who are saved, in other words, through the Church. God's plan ("that now, through the Church, the manifold wisdom of God should be made known") is to be realized, at least in part, through the Church's doing those works "which God prepared in advance."

The clause "which God prepared in advance" (or "beforehand," RSV) is crucial. It is already in the mind and plan of God that certain things which are part of the overall plan which God is accomplishing, should actually be done by the Church as good works. Thus redeemed men and women share in the realization of God's cosmic design. What God has set about to do since the creation of the world—"to bring all things in heaven and on earth together under one, even Christ"—is in part to be accomplished by the good works of the saved.[17] It is to be accomplished "through the church," not as so many isolated individuals, but precisely as "a new kind of community leading a radically new kind of life."[18]

But what, specifically, are these "good works, which God prepared in advance"? The Bible does not give us a specific catalog of kingdom tasks.[19] It is not difficult, however, to identify biblical criteria for determining which works are part of God's plan and which are opposed to it. There is a fivefold test that can be applied: Christians are accomplishing God's foreordained design whenever their works (1) spring from Christian love, (2) are based on obedience to the gospel and the stewardship of spiritual gifts, (3) are done in the name of Jesus, (4) work toward reconciliation, healing and beauty in the world, in whatever area, and (5) glorify the Father. Wherever a Christian is working in Jesus' name for reconciliation in the world, working to mend the brokenness of the world and to heal the sickness caused by the Fall, and where such activity springs from Christian love and a true sense of Christian vocation, there God is at work and there is a sign of the Kingdom.[20]

The task of the Church, then, and its place in God's cosmic design, is first of all genuinely to *be* the redeemed, messianic community, and secondly to *do* the works of God and carry on the works of Jesus. In truly being the community of Jesus' disciples the Church commits itself to a pattern of corporate life and a way of relating to one another which is a rejection of, and therefore a challenge to, the social and political structures of the world. In this way the Church's very existence becomes both prophetic and evangelistic. And in doing the works of God the Church repudiates the carnal weapons of the world (violence, force, deception, propaganda, manipulative technology) and employs the only weapons which are true to its own nature and the only weapons which, for it, are effective: truth, justice, peaceableness, faith, prayer and the Word of God (Eph. 6:14-18).

# 5
## THE MESSIANIC COMMUNITY

The Church is the agent of the Kingdom of God first of all through what it is. It best serves kingdom interests as the messianic community of God's people rather than as an ecclesiastical institution.

The book of Acts gives a balanced picture of the early Christian experience: evangelism and the Church, proclamation and community, witness and fellowship. The two primary concerns of the early church were the proclamation of the gospel and the edification of the Christian community. Evangelism sprang from the community, and the community grew through its witness. Evangelism was not merely something that individual Christians did; rather it was the natural result of the presence and influence of the Christian community in the world. The community gave credibility to the verbal proclamation.

**The Priority of Community** Proclamation presupposes a witnessing community. As John Howard Yoder has written, *Pragmatically it is self-evident that there can be no procedure of proclamation without a community, distinct from the rest of society, to do the proclaiming. Pragmatically it is just as clear that there can be no evangelistic call addressed to a person inviting him to enter into a* *new kind of fellowship and learning if there is not such a body of persons, again distinct from the totality of society, to whom he can come and with whom he can learn. . . . If it is not the case that there are in a given place men of various characters and origins who have been brought together in Jesus Christ, then there is not in that place the new humanity and in that place the gospel is not true. If, on the other hand, this miracle of new creation has occurred, then all the verbalizations and interpretations whereby this brotherhood communicates to the world around it are simply explications of the fact of its presence.*[1]

If Jesus Christ actually gave more time to preparing a community of disciples than to proclaiming the good news (which he did), then the contemporary Church must also recognize the importance of community for proclamation. I would emphasize the priority of community in two directions: in relation to the individual believer and in relation to witness.

In the first place community is important for the individual believer. Mainline Protestantism, from its structures to its hymns and gospel songs, has emphasized the individual over the community. It has had a keen sense of the individual person's responsibility before God but little corresponding sense of the communal life of the Christian. Too often the Church has been seen more as a mere collection of saved souls than as a community of interacting personalities. Christian growth has been a matter of individual soul culture rather than the building of the community of the Spirit. Saints who lived isolated, solitary lives were often placed on a pedestal above those whose lives were spent in true community. These tendencies, of course, were part of Protestantism's pre-Reformation heritage.

But four biblical truths should call us back to the priority of community: (1) the concept of the people of God, (2) the model of Christ with his disciples, (3) the example of the early church, and (4) the explicit teachings of Jesus and the apostles. Christ's statement, "Where two or three come together in my name, there am I with them" (Mt. 18:20) quite adequately defines the Church. Authentic Christian living is life in Christian community.

This does not mean, obviously, going to the opposite extreme and dissolving individual identity in the group. The individual emphasis is a biblical one, but a partial one.[2]

Spiritual growth occurs best in a caring community. There are spiritual truths I will never grasp and Christian standards I will never attain except as I share in community with other believers—and *this is God's plan.* The Holy Spirit ministers to us, in large measure, through each other. This is what Paul is talking about when he says "we will in all things grow up into him who is the Head, that is, Christ. From him the whole body, joined and held together by every supporting ligament, grows and builds itself up in love, as each part does its work" (Eph. 4:15-16). This interaction of the many members in one body is body life. Karl Barth rightly points out that when the New Testament speaks of upbuilding, it "speaks always of the upbuilding of the community. I can edify myself only as I edify the community."[3]

This has immediate implications for the evangelistic task. The individual believer's responsibility is first of all to the Christian community and to its head, Jesus Christ. The first task of every Christian is the edification of the community of believers. If we say that evangelism or soul winning is the first task of the believer, we do violence to the New Testament and place a burden on the backs of some believers that they are not able to bear. The idea that every Christian's first responsibility is to be a soul winner ignores the biblical teachings about spiritual gifts. Further, it puts all the emphasis at the one point of conversion and undervalues the upbuilding of the Church which is essential for effective evangelism and church growth.

This leads us to affirm, secondly, the priority of community in relation to witness. Fellowship and community life are necessary within the Church in order to equip Christians for their various kinds of witness and service. In one way or another every Christian is a witness in the world and must share his faith. But he can be an effective witness only as he experiences the enabling common life of the Church. And this common life is truly enabling only as the community becomes, through the indwelling of Christ and the exercise of spiritual gifts, the *koinonia* of the Holy Spirit.

This leads naturally to a discussion of the gifts of the Spirit in the Christian community. For gifts must be seen not as spiritual fringe benefits but as completely central to the life, experience and functioning of the Christian community.

**The Gifts of the Spirit**   Paul says, "There are different kinds of spiritual gifts, but the same Spirit" (1 Cor. 12:4). "We have different gifts, according to the grace given us" (Rom. 12:6). Likewise Peter: "Each one should use whatever spiritual gift he has received to serve others, faithfully administering God's grace in its various forms" (1 Pet. 4:10).[4]

For generations the subject of spiritual gifts was largely misunderstood or ignored by much of the Christian Church. The New Testament gives clear teachings regarding spiritual gifts and states emphatically that the exercise of such gifts is part of the normal life of the Christian community (1 Cor. 12—14). Yet even today many Christians either deny the validity of gifts, limiting them to the early church only, or reinterpret them in a way that robs them of their impact and sees them as synonymous with native abilities. This neglect and misunderstanding of gifts has produced a sometimes exaggerated emphasis on them among some groups. This reaction may represent God's judgment on mainline Protestantism for its neglect of this biblical truth. A polarization has resulted— one group denying or ignoring spiritual gifts, the other often overemphasizing them or elevating one or two gifts to the level of spiritual ID cards. Fortunately, we are beginning to see a new emphasis among both Pentecostals and non-Pentecostals on the fact that spiritual gifts must be understood in their biblical context, that is, as part of God's plan for the normal functioning of the Christian community.[5]

The basic question is not whether specific spiritual gifts, such as those of apostle, prophet or tongues-speaking, are valid today. The question is whether the Spirit still "gives gifts to men," and the answer is yes. Precisely which gifts he gives in any particular age is God's prerogative, and we should not prejudge God. Interpretations as to specific gifts may vary. But we have no biblical warrant to restrict the *charismata* to the early church nor to ban any specific gift today. Arguments against gifts generally arise from secondary, not biblical, considerations and a fear of excesses or abuses.

My own study of the Church in the New Testament convinces me that we can understand God's plan for the Church only as we give proper attention to spiritual gifts. This is no strange doctrine but something the early church understood very well. In Ephesians spiritual gifts form the connecting link between Paul's statement of God's cosmic plan for the Church and his description of normal local church life: "There is one body and one Spirit. . . . But to each one of us grace has been given as Christ apportioned it. . . . It was he who gave some to be apostles, some to be prophets, some to be evangelists, and some to be pastors and teachers" (Eph. 4:4, 7, 11). Having been saved by grace, "we are God's workmanship, created in Christ Jesus to do good works, which God prepared in advance for us to do" (Eph. 2:10). There is a link between these foreordained "good works" and spiritual gifts, for it is principally through the exercise of spiritual gifts that the individual accomplishes those good works which make up God's cosmic plan.

The life and growth of the early church can be seen best as a community of Spirit-filled Christians exercising their spiritual gifts. Some, like Peter, Paul, Barnabas, Silas, Philip and Apollos, used their gifts in direct proclamation of the gospel to the world. Others used their gifts to sustain the internal life of the Church—such as, for instance, Timothy, Ananias (Acts 9:10), Mary the mother of Mark (Acts 12:12), Phoebe (Rom. 16:1-2), Priscilla and Aquila (Rom. 16:3), and many others too numerous to mention.

Paul clearly states that his "gift of God's grace" as an apostle was "to preach to the Gentiles the unsearchable riches of Christ, and to make plain to everyone my administration of this mystery" of the gospel (Eph. 3:7-9). Paul was an apostle; this was his spiritual gift. It involved for him evangelism and church planting as well as teaching and spiritual oversight. He was effective because he was exercising the gift and calling he had received from God the Spirit.

Philip was an evangelist. Agabus was a prophet; we have no evidence he was an evangelist. Dorcas "was always doing good and helping the poor" (Acts 9:36); that is how she exercised her spiritual gifts. Lydia of Philippi led a prayer group and practiced the gift of hospitality (Acts 16:13-15). Silas was a prophet (Acts 15:32), and Phoebe was a deaconess (Rom. 16:1).[6] And so on throughout the early church. Not all of these were evangelists, but all were witnesses to the grace of God. And each one, in his or her own way, was useful in the witness of the Church.

New Testament examples reveal two directions of spiritual gifts: outward, ministry in the world; and inward, ministry within the Church. Both are important and both are needed, for proclamation and service must grow out of the Church's experience of community.

Peter's teaching in 1 Peter 4:10-11 gives perhaps the best summary of biblical teaching concerning spiritual gifts. He says, "Each one should use whatever spiritual gift [gift of grace, *charisma*] he has received to serve others, faithfully administering God's grace [*charis*] in its various forms. If anyone speaks, he should do it as one speaking the very words of God. If anyone serves, he should do it with the strength God provides, so that in all things God may be praised through Jesus Christ." This passage is important because it shows that spiritual gifts were not just Paul's idea but were commonly accepted and understood in the early church. Hebrews 2:4 (assuming Paul is not the author) is important for the same reason: "God also testified to it by signs, wonders and various miracles, and gifts of the Holy Spirit distributed according to his will."[7]

Peter assumes that each believer has received some spiritual gift, some specific distribution of God's manifold grace, and says this gift is to be used to glorify God. Peter cites only two examples: the ministry of the Word ("if anyone speaks") and practical service ("if anyone serves," *diakonei*). Obviously, this is not to limit spiritual gifts to just two. Rather Peter is speaking of all spiritual gifts and divides them broadly into two categories, verbal proclamation and practical service, just as the twelve disciples did in Acts 6.[8] This is a natural and practical division, not a rigid technical or hierarchical one. Peter is simply saying, "Whatever gift you have received—whether to speak or to serve—use it faithfully, as a good steward of God's grace, in order that God may be glorified" (which is always the final purpose of spiritual gifts).

**Understanding Specific Gifts**  With this background, we can now look at some of the more detailed lists of spiritual gifts. The way these gifts are mentioned in the New Testament and the variety of Greek words employed should warn us against a rigid or narrow interpretation. The New Testament emphasis is on the diversity of the Spirit's gifts. Each believer receives the grace (*charis*) that the individual—and the Church—needs.

The most important Pauline passages on gifts are Romans 12:6-8, 1 Corinthians 12:8-10 and 12:28, and Ephesians 4:11-12. Here are four different listings of the gifts of the Spirit. While the lists are essentially similar, Paul may have had something slightly different in mind in 1 Corinthians 12:28 and Ephesians 4:11-12 than in Romans 12:6-8 and 1 Corinthians 12:8-10. In the latter two passages the emphasis is on the fact of the gifts themselves and the resultant diversity within the unity of the body of Christ. Paul speaks here of prophecy, teaching, healing and so on rather than of prophets, teachers, healers and so forth.

In contrast Paul has something else in mind in Ephesians 4:11-12 and 1 Corinthians 12:28. His concern is clear in the latter passage: "And in the church God has appointed...." Paul's emphasis is not primarily on the gifts themselves in these two passages but on *the order of the church.* He focuses attention on the means God has provided for the proper functioning of the gifts within the Christian community.

Placing these two passages side by side gives us a composite picture of church order according to biblical and charismatic principles, and suggests a functional distinction between two kinds of gifts:

| *1 Corinthians 12:28* | *Ephesians 4:11-12 (RSV)* |
|:---:|:---:|
| Apostles, prophets, teachers | Apostles, prophets, evangelists, pastors, teachers |
| then | for |
| workers of miracles, healers, helpers, etc. | the equipment of the saints for their work of ministry |

We note that common to these two lists are apostles, prophets and teachers. In Ephesians are added evangelists and pastors, which may be considered the further subdividing of those included in 1 Corinthians as apostles, prophets and teachers.

In 1 Corinthians 12:28, after mentioning *"first* of all apostles, *second* prophets, *third* teachers," Paul goes on to mention several other gifts: *"then* workers of miracles, also those having gifts of healing, those able to help others, those with gifts of administration, and finally those speaking in different kinds of tongues." A natural division is evident here. This is a functional distinction between the basic leadership or enabling gifts and the great variety of other, more specific gifts which the Spirit gives.

Note that Paul is not referring here to an organized, fixed hierarchy in the Church, though sometimes such an interpretation is read into the text. Rather, Paul is showing that God himself has provided for order by giving, within each local congregation and in the Church in general, persons capable of exercising the various necessary functions.

We see, then, that the basic leadership gifts of apostle, prophet, evangelist, pastor and teacher are given to the Church to exercise an equipping ministry, preparing each believer for a specific ministry. And what is this work of ministry? For each member it is different, but we see some of the things it involves: healing, helping, administration, prophecy. In all cases the goal is the same, that is, "that the church may be edified" (1 Cor. 14:5), that "all reach unity in the faith and in the knowledge of the Son of God and become mature, attaining the full measure of perfection found in Christ" (Eph. 4:13), "so that in all things God may be praised through Jesus Christ" (1 Pet. 4:11).

**Charismatic Leadership**    How are we to understand these enabling functions of apostle, prophet, evangelist, pastor and teacher today?

In the first place there is a difference in the scope or sphere of action of these various gifts. William Barclay summarizes the biblical and historical evidence concerning leadership in the early church as follows:

*In the early Church there were three kinds of office-bearers. There were a few whose writ and whose authority ran throughout the whole church [apostles]. There were many whose ministry was not confined to one place, but who carried out a wandering ministry, going wherever the Spirit moved them, and where God sent them [prophets and evangelists]. There were some whose ministry was a local ministry which was confined to the one congregation and to the one place [pastors and teachers].*[9]

The wide-ranging leadership role of the apostles is clear throughout the New Testament. Although the gift of prophecy was often exercised within local congregations (1 Cor. 14), many prophets and evangelists had an itinerant ministry something like that of Old Testament prophets (Acts 11:27-28; 21:8-10; Eph. 3:5; 2 Pet. 3:2; Rev. 18:20). Unlike the apostles, they were not overseers. Finally, the ministry of pastors and teachers was confined basically to local congregations (Acts 13:1; 20:17-20). Elders are sometimes spoken of as pastors or teachers (Acts 20:17-30; 1 Tim. 5:17; 1 Pet. 5:1-3).

The pattern of leadership that actually existed in the early church formed the basis for what Paul later taught concerning the gifts in his Epistles. For this reason Paul's teaching in Ephesians and 1 Corinthians should take priority over the descriptions in Acts of the various leaders which were in fact emerging. In his evangelism Paul saw the need for leadership and, led by the Spirit, appointed elders in the churches he founded. Later, writing to these churches, Paul reflected on what had happened and gave an interpretation showing what God had done: "In the church God has appointed first of all apostles, second prophets, third teachers." Under divine inspiration Paul gives this explanation, showing that God has acted, and will act, to provide leadership. And Paul shows that this leadership is to be understood in terms of spiritual gifts: he gave "some to be apostles, some to be prophets, some to be evangelists, some to be pastors and teachers." These are not all the gifts, but they are the leadership or enabling gifts.

Paul's interpretation here becomes, then, not merely description but also revelation—the revealing of God's plan, his *oikonomia*, for leadership and order in the Church. Whether we call them elders, deacons, pastors, bishops or superintendents, the fact is that God provides for leadership in the Church through the exercise of the gifts of the Spirit. This is God's ecclesiology.

Our understanding would be clearer if we remember the fundamental meaning of words that have come to be known only as titles. These terms were understood in New Testament days not as ecclesiastical titles but as practical functions. Some of these terms had been used for leaders in Judaism (for instance, elder), while others were common in Greek culture. But each term was taken over by the church because it described an emerging leadership function. Note the terms in Table 1.[10]

| English Term | Greek Word | Basic Meaning | English Derivatives |
|---|---|---|---|
| elder | *presbuteros* | an older, more mature person or leader | presbyter, priest |
| servant, minister, deacon, deaconess | *diakonos* | one who serves | deacon, deaconess |
| pastor, shepherd | *poimēn* | shepherd | |
| bishop, overseer | *episkopos* | overseer | bishop, episcopate |
| apostle | *apostolos* | messenger, one who is sent or commissioned | apostle |
| evangelist | *euaggelistēs* | teller of good news | evangelist |
| teacher, master | *didaskalos* | teacher | (didactic) |

**Table 1. Roots of Ecclesiastical Titles**

These terms were used by the early church to designate the leaders God's Spirit was raising up. They were more descriptive than prescriptive. Taken together, they do not represent a fixed hierarchy of offices to be filled, but rather indicate the leadership functions that were carried out by men and women God raised up. This is what is meant by *charismatic leadership*— leadership inspired by God's Spirit, endowed with needed graces or charisms and appropriately recognized by the believing community.

John Howard Yoder has made a detailed study of charismatic leadership, biblically understood, which bears quoting at some length for the light it sheds on the nature of leadership in general and especially on the question of the New Testament vocabulary of ministry.[11] Yoder notes that every society makes a place for the "professional religionist" who is supported by the community and takes care of its religious functions. As the Church strays from biblical principles it becomes like other religions and cultural systems and accepts the professional religionist's role and powers.

If *we come to the New Testament with this "professional religionist" view of ministry, asking "What is said on this subject?" then we can add together some things which Paul said about himself as apostle, some things he wrote to Timothy and Titus about themselves, some other things he wrote to them about bishops and deacons, some things Acts reports about the leaders in Jerusalem and Antioch, salt the mixture with some reminiscences from the Old Testament, and come up with a quite impressive package as the "Biblical View of Ministry."*[12]

If we take the New Testament on its own terms, however, and analyze its own vocabulary of ministry, we find a "resounding negation" of the assumptions underlying the professional religionist view.

Yoder points out that "there is a considerable number of distinguishable ministries" or functions in the New Testament as well as "a diversity in the number, naming and interrelation of these offices." Further, "there is a certain *logical* priority in the naming of the apostle and prophet, but there is no hierarchy of value. . . . There is no hint of a 'ladder' whereby the same individual might progress 'upward' from one office to another."[13]

*Let us take quite seriously the warning of 1 Cor. 12 against trying to establish a hierarchy of values among the varied gifts. This warning is the point of the passage: that there are many gifts is not the chapter's message, for that is self-evident, at least in Corinth. Paul's whole concern is that it be recognized that all these many gifts have the same source, and that all are (each in its place) of the same value.*[14]

Concerning the New Testament vocabulary of leadership: *There seems to be a clustering of three terms used for the same office. "Elder" is derived from synagogue usage, "overseer" (bishop) is a functional description, and "shepherd" a figurative one. The three terms appear synonymously in Acts 20 and 1 Pet. 5, and bishop/elder in Tit. 1. They constituted the collegial leadership of the self-governing local congregation. There are several of these men in a given congregation.*[15]

As to the supposed "office" of deacon, Yoder observes that in the New Testament the word *diakonos* normally "means simply 'one who serves' with no clear implication of office."[16] One must therefore be extremely hesitant to assume the so-called office of deacon was a fixed leadership role in the New Testament.

All leadership in the Church, therefore, is based on spiritual gifts. Biblically, one simply cannot make "the assumption that charisma and office are on two levels, the one spontaneous and the other fixed, the one lively and the other reliable. . . . The only way to define 'office' in such a way as to bear no relationship at all to 'gift' is to make a given task so objective, formal, impersonal that it must and can be discharged by someone whom God has not prepared for it."[17]

Yoder's analysis shows how careful one must be not to read back into the New Testament rigid, once-for-all leadership structures which simply are not there. In fact the New Testament description of the Church as the messianic community undercuts the very basis of any institutional/hierarchical view and puts ministry on a charismatic/organic basis. The important teachings from the New Testament are: (1) God provided the necessary leaders, (2) this leadership was seen in terms of the exercise of spiritual gifts, and (3) there was great flexibility and fluidity in the way these leadership functions operated and were understood in the early church.

This flexibility and fluidity in leadership terminology is borne out by biblical examples. Philip, for instance, was recognized as both a "table server" and an evangelist (Acts 6:5; 21:8). Silas, Paul's companion, was one of the "leading men" and also a prophet (Acts 15:22, 32). The church at Antioch had "prophets and teachers" (Acts 13:1). The leaders assembled at the Council of Jerusalem are repeatedly called "apostles and elders" (Acts 15); undoubtedly many of these elders were the pastors and teachers from various local congregations. Writing to the church in Philippi, Paul addressed himself to "the saints . . ., together with the overseers and deacons" (Phil. 1:1). It appears that elders, deacons and bishops (overseers) were appointed leaders who were recognized as having one or more of the leadership gifts cited by Paul in 1 Corinthians 12 and Ephesians 4.[18]

The clearest biblical teaching concerning leadership in the Christian community is the fact that there are basic enabling gifts of apostle, prophet, evangelist, pastor and teacher. Let us look briefly at each of these functions.

*Apostles.* Paul was very conscious of being an apostle and of the apostolic ministry in general. The Church is "built on the foundation of the apostles and prophets, with Christ Jesus himself as the chief cornerstone" (Eph. 2:20). God's plan through the Church "has now been revealed by the Spirit to God's holy apostles and prophets" (Eph. 3:5).

In the early church an apostle was one recognized as having a place of pre-eminent leadership and authority in the Church. Often he played a key role in cross-cultural evangelism. The original apostles, that is, the chosen disciples of Jesus, plus Paul, were recognized as having particular authority because of their closeness to Christ: they had seen him and were witnesses of his resurrection, although (significantly) in the case of Paul this was by vision and by direct revelation not by physical association.

But did apostleship continue beyond the New Testament period? Because of the obvious uniqueness of the original apostles, some have argued that apostles no longer exist today. But this conclusion runs counter to biblical evidence and makes too sharp a break between the original apostles and the church leaders who followed them.

The word *apostle (apostolos)* or *apostles* occurs eighty-one times in the New Testament. As we examine these occurrences, several conclusions emerge.

First and most obviously, the "apostles" were the twelve disciples especially chosen by Jesus. The word occurs with this meaning seven times in the Gospels, as well as in Acts 1:2 and possibly Jude 17.

Second, *apostles* designates the principal leaders of the early church in the book of Acts. In Acts 1 Matthias was chosen to replace Judas and "was added to the eleven apostles" (Acts 1:26). The frequent mention of apostles in Acts 1 through 6 (fourteen times) quite clearly refers to "the Twelve" (Acts 6:2) —the original eleven, plus Matthias.

But beginning with Acts 8, we can no longer be sure that *apostles* refers only to the Twelve. Gradually the meaning of the term seems to expand to include other emerging leaders. With time not only Paul and Barnabas (Acts 14:4, 14) but also James, Jesus' brother (Gal. 1:19), Apollos (1 Cor. 4:9) and Silas (1 Thess. 2:7) were called apostles. Adronicus and Junias (Rom. 16:7), the latter possibly a woman, seem also to have been considered apostles.

In the book of Acts, *apostles* in the broader sense of general church leaders—not necessarily restricted to the Twelve—appears twenty-four times. The identity of the "apostles and elders" in Acts 15 is not specified, and we have no solid grounds for assuming *apostles* here means the Twelve only, especially considering the prominence of James at the Jerusalem council (Acts 15:13).[19]

Beyond these meanings, referring to the Twelve and then to an expanding group of church leaders, the New Testament also uses *apostle* in a still broader sense as referring to messengers or missionaries. This is the case, for example, in John 13:16, 2 Corinthians 8:23 (RSV) and Philippians 2:25.

It is against this background of early church usage that we should understand Paul's designation of *apostle* as a spiritual gift (1 Cor. 12:28-29; Eph. 4:11). We have no warrant for restricting the meaning here to the original Twelve.[20] Surely we can recognize a unique, unrepeatable apostleship in that first group of apostles. But already in Paul's day there were other apostles. What Paul is indicating is not the original Twelve, but rather the function of apostle which God has given as a permanent aspect of the charismatic nature of the Church. Nothing in Paul's treatment of spiritual gifts suggests that he was describing a pattern for the early church only. Quite the opposite. For Paul the Church is a growing, grace-filled body, and apostles are a permanent part of that body's life.

It cannot be successfully maintained, therefore, that the apostolic ministry passed away with the death of the original Twelve. Nor is there biblical evidence, conversely, that the apostolic ministry was transmitted formally and hierarchically down through the history of the Church. Rather, Scripture teaches that the Spirit continually and charismatically gives to the Church the function of apostle.

Apostles, then, usually are (1) general leaders for the Church (2) whose place and authority are recognized throughout the Church (3) because of a general conviction that the Spirit of God has raised them up. They are general leaders whose authority is based in their being raised up by God and in their faithfulness to revealed truth, that is, the Bible. Their authority is contingent upon their faithfulness as witnesses; ceasing to witness faithfully to the truth of God's revelation, they cease to have authority.

Apostles today, then, are the Church's general leaders, those who have responsibility for the general oversight of the Church. These are the leaders God chooses as witnesses to his revelation and guardians of that revelation; leaders responsible for the good order of the Church.

How do truly divinely-appointed apostles come to be recognized and to exercise their function within the Church? This raises the question of organizational structure which the New Testament does not deal with explicitly. Presumably a variety of organizational patterns are possible, provided such forms do not violate the very biblical principles which make leadership valid and functional. It makes little difference biblically whether apostles today are called bishops, superintendents, moderators, presidents or what have you.[21] It is important that the structure be sufficiently flexible and open so that the true apostles can exercise their New Testament function (admittedly a rare thing in many church structures) and, similarly, that the means of appointing these leaders permit and encourage a sensitivity to the voice of the Holy Spirit so that those chosen are indeed the ones God is choosing.

It should be obvious that there is no inherent authority in the *office* of apostle, simply because the apostolate is not an office to be given to a person chosen by the Church.[22] Apostleship is a *function*, a gift. God has not established the office of apostle, prophet, evangelist and so forth. This would be to think in static, institutional terms. Rather, "his gifts were that some should be apostles, prophets, evangelists." The gift from God is persons, not offices. This distinction is useful today because of the tendency to think in institutional and organizational, rather than personal and charismatic (and thus biblical) terms.[23] Thus apostolic authority can neither be conferred nor transferred, except as this is done by the Holy Spirit.[24]

*Prophets.* From the New Testament and early Christian writings we know something of the function of prophet in the primitive church. William Barclay notes, "The prophets were wanderers throughout the Church. Their message was held to be not the result of thought and study, but the direct result of the Holy Spirit. . . . They went from Church to Church proclaiming the will of God as God had told it to them."[25] It is obvious by Paul's usage of the term in Ephesians and elsewhere that prophets, like apostles, were recognized as having a general and pre-eminent ministry throughout the Church. In a somewhat more restricted sense, prophecy was also a gift often exercised by individuals within the local church (1 Cor. 14:26-40).

Who are the present-day prophets? Often they are the so-called charismatic leaders (in the sociological sense) that spring up in the Church. Almost every denomination and movement has in its history those Spirit-inspired persons whom all recognize as leaders and men and women of God, even though they may have no official church office. They generally are not administrators or overseers. Many times these persons become the traveling evangelists and special speakers in the Church, or they may found special organizations or movements within or parallel to the organized church (for example, youth movements or missionary organizations). Or they may eventually be tapped for denominational leadership as a bishop or general officer. More frequently, however, the charismatic leader is passed over in choosing such officers because he is too independent and unpredictable for the office. Or, if actually chosen, he may refuse the office because he sees it as too limiting. These people, if truly people of God, are too big for the office previously created. (A good contemporary example of this was E. Stanley Jones in the Methodist Church, who refused the office of bishop.)

There is biblical provision, then, for "individualistic," so-called charismatic leaders who emerge within the Christian community. If they are genuinely men or women of God, filled with the Spirit (for false prophets also abound), they may be prophets whom God is raising up. Their ministry will be one of direct relationship to God and to the Church. They will have all the power—and all the possibility of being unconventional and unpredictable—of true prophets. They will also be subject to the dangers of extremism since their message comes directly from God and the temptation will be to speak on their own and claim to be speaking for God. In all these respects we see a direct relationship to the Old Testament prophets.

The prophet in the Church may or may not be an official leader. That is incidental. A prophet is appointed by God's Holy Spirit, independent of any official position. If the Church is spiritual, it will recognize the authenticity and immediacy of the prophetic gift.

As in the Bible, so in the Church: the prophet is God's instrument speaking directly to his people (and, perhaps, secondarily to the world) with encouragement, exhortation, warning or judgment, according to the situation. The validity of his or her message does not depend upon approval or acceptance by the Church. The message is valid only, however, if in harmony with the Bible, because the Spirit of God is a Spirit of order, not confusion. He does not contradict himself.

So the Church does not choose its prophets. It only recognizes them and listens to them. It may, in one way or another, sustain them. And the appearance of true prophets in the Church, we may be certain, is a sign of God's operation among his people for he has promised to raise them up. Why should we be startled when they appear?

*Evangelists.* Surprisingly, the term *evangelist* does not occur frequently in the New Testament. The only occurrences are in Ephesians 4:11, Acts 21:8 ("Philip the evangelist") and 2 Timothy 4:5 ("do the work of an evangelist"). Why so few references? The answer is that Paul, and the New Testament church in general, did not conceive of evangelism as primarily the work of specialists. Evangelism happened; it was the natural expression of the life of the Church. There was little need either to exhort people to evangelize or to raise up a special class of evangelists because new Christians went everywhere "gossiping" the good news about Jesus.

But if this is so, why then does Paul even mention evangelists at all? The answer probably lies in the simple fact that people who were gifted as evangelists, and recognized as such (in distinction to apostles and prophets with whom they presumably had much in common), had arisen in the Church. Paul recognized these men and women as being within God's ecclesiology. The growth of a healthy church does not depend on the work of evangelists, however, for the Church is a witnessing community. But a healthy church may properly have and profitably use such "specialists." This, apparently, was the situation in the early church.

Apostles were also evangelists (Peter, Paul) but Paul refers especially to those whose function was limited more or less exclusively to evangelism. Particularly, in distinction from the apostles, the evangelists did not have responsibility for the general oversight of the Church, although their function may have included the proclamation of the good news to and within the Christian community as well as outside it.[26] The primary function was always proclamation, "bearing the good news."

Thus evangelists exercise a legitimate function within the Church, and we may expect God to raise up evangelists in our day both within the local church and more generally in the Church at large. The Church should be alert to recognize these people and should encourage and facilitate their work. It should not, however, fall into the error of thinking that only such evangelists have responsibility for evangelism. All Christians must witness in one way or another, and many Christians will have a gift in the area of evangelism, even if they are not specifically called as evangelists.

*Pastors and Teachers.* These may be thought of as one group or as two distinct groups; some scholars put them together as pastor-teachers. In practice it makes little difference, since these distinctions are not rigid. The pastoral and teaching ministries are two more or less distinct but overlapping functions. And these, for the most part, involve local leaders whose ministry is to and within the local congregation.

There is nothing here (or elsewhere in the New Testament) to suggest that *pastor* in the early church had anything like the highly specialized and professional sense it has come to have in modern Protestantism. Ephesians 4:11 is, in fact, the only occurrence of the word *pastors* in the New Testament sense of congregational leaders, although the idea of the congregation as a flock to be cared for occurs in John 21:16, Acts 20:28 and 1 Peter 5:2.

We are left, then, not with a pastoral *office* as such but simply with the pastoral *function.* This shepherding function is necessary for the edification and growth of the Church. In the normal (that is, biblical) local congregation, God will raise up those (not just one) whose ministry is to shepherd the flock. This is a spiritual gift.

Shepherding includes teaching. The teaching ministry was and is essential in the Church. Paul elsewhere shows his concern for the teaching ministry (1 Tim. 3:2; 4:11-12; 2 Tim. 2:2) and himself dedicated time to teaching converts in the cities he evangelized.

There is much to be taught. There is doctrinal teaching, which is essential; teaching in the disciplines of the Christian life; training in evangelism; and Bible teaching in general. Whatever else may be taught in the local church, this surely must be the core curriculum.

**The New Testament Pattern and Ours**  These then are the four or five basic leadership or enabling ministries in the New Testament—apostles, prophets, evangelists, pastors and teachers. They are God's gift to the Church "to prepare God's people for works of service."

It would be well if each present-day denomination and each local church would take this list and lay it alongside a list of the leaders prescribed by the church's official organizational structure and, before God, make a comparison. Are the lists comparable at all? How does the church actually function compared with what the Word of God says? Is the practical application of Ephesians 4:11 and 1 Corinthians 12:28 even possible in our church, given its present structure? If not, what would God have us do? In some cases the choice may actually be either thorough changes in the organizational structure or an effective cancellation of the Word of God at this point.

What is the relationship between these basic leadership or equipping gifts and the ministry gifts of the Christian community in general? Our two scriptures make it plain: these leadership gifts are to equip the saints for their work of ministry, and these works of ministry involve (representatively, not exclusively) the exercise of such gifts as healing, prophecy, miracles, tongues, helping, administering and interpretation of tongues (Eph. 4:11; 1 Cor. 12). The goal is the edification of the Church, and thereby the glorification of God and the accomplishing of his cosmic plan.

The pattern of leadership and ministry outlined above allows for no rigid distinction between clergy and laity. The New Testament simply does not speak in terms of two classes of Christians—"ministers" and "laymen"—as we do today. According to the Bible, the people (*laos*, "laity") of God comprise all Christians, and all Christians through the exercise of spiritual gifts have some "work of ministry." So if we wish to be biblical, we will have to say that all Christians are laymen

(God's people) and all are ministers. The clergy-laity dichotomy is unbiblical and therefore invalid. It grew up as an accident of church history and actually marked a drift away from biblical faithfulness.

A professional, distinct priesthood did exist in Old Testament days. But in the New Testament this priesthood is replaced by two truths: Jesus Christ is our great high priest, and the Church is a kingdom of priests (Heb. 4:14; 8:1; 1 Pet. 2:9; Rev. 1:6).

The New Testament doctrine of ministry rests therefore not on the clergy-laity distinction but on the twin and complementary pillars of the priesthood of all believers and the gifts of the Spirit.[27] Today, four centuries after the Reformation, the full implications of this Protestant affirmation have yet to be worked out. The clergy-laity dichotomy is a direct carry-over from pre-Reformation Roman Catholicism and a throwback to the Old Testament priesthood. It is one of the principal obstacles to the Church effectively being God's agent of the Kingdom today because it creates the false idea that only "holy men," namely, ordained ministers, are really qualified and responsible for leadership and significant ministry. In the New Testament there are functional distinctions between various kinds of ministries but no hierarchical division between clergy and laity.

Because we repeatedly read this dichotomy into the Bible, it has become for us a great obstacle to a biblical understanding of the Church. Some fundamental rethinking is overdue precisely at this point.

**The Messianic Role**   The early Christian affirmation that "Jesus is Lord" must be the cry of the Church today. The promised Messiah has come, and the Church is both his bride and body. It is that new social reality, that "new creation" in the world which is called to demonstrate the true character of the coming Kingdom.

This is why the Church is truly the agent of God's cosmic plan only as it is truly the community of God's people. As an ecclesiastical institution the Church can show little, if anything, of the Kingdom. But as the messianic community functioning as a charismatic body, it can and does reveal the true nature of the Kingdom and hastens its coming.

# three

## EMBODYING
## THE KINGDOM COMMUNITY

I TELL YOU THE TRUTH, UNLESS A MAN IS BORN
OF WATER AND THE SPIRIT, HE CANNOT
ENTER THE KINGDOM OF GOD.
(JN. 3:5)

WHERE TWO OR THREE COME TOGETHER IN MY
NAME, THERE AM I WITH THEM.
(MT. 18:20)

# 6
## THE KINGDOM
## MANDATE

The very existence of the Christian community is a sign of the Kingdom of God. But, as we have seen, the Church also is responsible to walk in those good works which God prepared before hand. It must continue in the world the works of Jesus Christ.

The role of the Church is both evangelistic and prophetic, without being exclusively one or the other. Authentic evangelization is itself prophetic, and a truly prophetic voice is evangelistic. The Church is called to be prophetically evangelistic and evangelistically prophetic.

In one sense evangelism is good news and prophecy is bad news. Evangelism and prophecy make up the positive and negative charges of the Church's spiritual power. Evangelism proclaims the offer of forgiveness, new life in Christ and new lifestyle in Christian community. Prophecy proclaims that even if this offer is rejected, God is still sovereign and will finally establish his Kingdom in righteousness and in judgment. Evangelism is the offer of present salvation; prophecy is the assurance of final judgment.

There are many ways the Church's kingdom tasks may be viewed. One might simply list the kinds of things the Church should be doing. Or the Church's responsibilities in relation to the individual, the family, the State, the environment and the world might each be considered. In this chapter, however, I have chosen simply to outline the Church's evangelistic and prophetic roles while emphasizing that this implies no dichotomy between the two.

**The Evangelistic Mandate**   Just as most biblical images for the Church imply life, so do they suggest *growth* or *reproduction*. It is of the nature of the Church to grow and multiply itself, just as God's plan has always involved the charge, "Be fruitful and multiply" (Gen. 1:28). To this life principle is added the urgency of the Great Commission, the words of the risen Christ.

The mandate for proclamation and witness is central in God's cosmic plan, for this plan centers in what God is doing for people (the redemption that brings eternal salvation and builds the Church). And it should be equally clear that the evangelistic task is not merely the task of individual believers but is a function of the Church as the community of God's people.

Two of the most characteristic words in Acts are *marturein*, "to bear witness" (from which comes the English word *martyr*) and *euaggelizesthai*, "to proclaim the gospel" (from which comes the English word *evangelize*). Both these words occur in one form or another over twenty times in Acts. The great concern and dynamic of the early church was to tell the good news about Jesus and the resurrection; to bear witness to what had been seen, heard and experienced.[1]

Some writers on the Church have emphasized the word *kerygma*, referring to the preaching of the early church. It is clear from the New Testament documents, however, that the essential message of the first Christians was more than a fixed kerygmatic formula, and it was more than formal preaching. Most certainly it was more than the disciples' proclamation of a subjective, existential interpretation of the "resurrection event." Rather the *kerygma* or preaching was grounded in the telling of the good news about the resurrection of Christ which the first Christians had witnessed. Both the clear meaning of the book of Acts and a more technical word study reveal the priority of witness and gospel proclamation in the early church.[2]

Michael Green suggests in *Evangelism in the Early Church* that *marturia* rather than *kerygma* (witness rather than preaching) should probably be considered the characteristic word of New Testament evangelism.[3] When the first Christians proclaimed the good news they were witnesses, and when they died as martyrs (*martures*) they were witnesses. The evangelistic task involved—and involves today—witness both by word and by life. The early Christians had seen and experienced (1 Jn. 1:1-3) the good news; their eyewitness formed the basis for preaching.

The evangelistic task of the Church is to proclaim the good news of salvation in Jesus Christ throughout the world, making disciples and building the Church. It is to fulfill the Great Commission of Matthew 28:19-20, Mark 16:15 and Acts 1:8. Although the role of the Church in God's plan does not end with the evangelistic task, it begins here; the realization of God's purpose depends on this task being carried out.

I would quickly make three points here. First, *evangelism is the first priority of the Church's ministry in the world.* This is true for several reasons: the clear biblical mandate for evangelism; the centrality and necessity of personal conversion in God's plan; the reality of judgment; the fact that changed persons are necessary to change society; the fact that the Christian community exists and expands only as evangelism is carried out. The Church that fails to evangelize is both biblically unfaithful and strategically shortsighted.

Some object to what they call the "prioritization of evangelism" as betraying the wholeness of the gospel. Should evangelism really be put first? The basic priority of the Church is to glorify God. That takes precedence even over evangelism, although evangelism may be a way of glorifying God. But evangelism can be either authentic or a betrayal of the gospel depending on how it is carried out. An evangelism which focuses exclusively on souls or on an otherworldly transaction which makes no real difference here and now is unfaithful to the gospel. An evangelism of cheap grace which does not call for true, present allegiance to Jesus as Lord is not true evangelism.

What is needed is the kind of radical evangelism which calls people to Jesus Christ and his body and to identification with the people Jesus showed concern for. Men and women need to have their sins forgiven; they need to be born again through the regenerating power of the Holy Spirit. But they must know that this regeneration means loyalty to Jesus as Lord as well as Savior. Evangelism must involve, says Gilbert James, "a reuniting of the personal and social aspects of Christian experience that emphasizes total obedience to Christ as Lord in every category of life."[4]

Second, *evangelism is essentially witness.* That is, the various elements that make up evangelism spring from experiencing what God has done in Christ and in the Church. Evangelism is bearing witness, in various ways and through various means, to what God has done.

To say evangelism is essentially witness is not to play down or deny the verbal proclamation of a specific message with specific content. Rather, it is to emphasize that evangelism is both the preaching of the good news and the demonstration of the good news.

This witness is giving testimony to what God has done in history, supremely in the life, death and resurrection of Jesus Christ. It is the proclamation and demonstration of the liberation Jesus brings. This liberation is first of all spiritual and moral: man is liberated from the power of sin and brought into fellowship with God and with fellow believers. It is also social and political, though not in the sense that it requires or justifies a particular political program. Because the Church is a collective, social reality, it is (when faithful to the gospel) both a political fact and a political challenge.[5]

Third, *witness is a function of the Church-as-community.* If the New Testament shows us the Peters and Pauls going abroad preaching the gospel, it also presents us with the reality of the Christian community which served both as the enabler and the verification of gospel proclamation. The New Testament evangelists were faithful verbal witnesses largely because the Christian community was a faithful witness through its common life and its action in the world. Witness and community go together. A concept of evangelism which sees isolated individuals independently scattering the Word throughout the world, without regard for the life and witness of the Christian community, is truncated and self-defeating. Evangelism takes place through the life of the witnessing community (Jn. 13:35).

**Church-Based Evangelism**    If the vision of the Church presented throughout this book is valid, then biblical evangelism must be church-based evangelism. That is, evangelism should spark church growth, and the life and witness of the Church should produce evangelism. In this sense the Church is both the *agent* and the *goal* of evangelism.

Church-centered evangelism is evangelism which builds the Church. It springs from the life and witness of the Christian community and results in the growth and reproduction of the community in an ongoing process.

Missiologist C. Peter Wagner and others have rightly criticized views of evangelism which do not go far enough in the direction of church growth. Speaking of "presence evangelism" and "proclamation evangelism," Wagner insists that neither is adequate, for evangelism must include persuasion. Christian presence must be the basis for Christian proclamation, and these together persuade people to come to Christ:

Presence → Proclamation → Persuasion

Biblical evangelism is concerned with results; it is concerned to reap, not just to sow. In this view, the ultimate aim of evangelism is to make disciples.[6]

But is it enough even to say the ultimate goal of evangelism is to make disciples? While making disciples certainly implies the formation and edification of the Christian community, this is only implicit, not explicit. To do justice to the biblical understanding of the Church we must go one step further and say that *the goal of evangelism is the formation of the Christian community.*[7] It is making disciples and, further, forming these disciples into living cells of the body of Christ, new expressions of the community of God's people. Church-based evangelism is concerned, then, with propagation (in the fundamental sense of reproduction or multiplication by generation) as well as with persuasion. Thus church-based evangelism can be more fully illustrated by this diagram:

Presence → Proclamation → Persuasion → Propagation

In this process, propagation or reproduction feeds into a continuous cycle which, empowered by the Holy Spirit, makes the Church a dynamic, living organism. The goal of evangelism therefore is the formation of the Christian community, the *koinonia* of the Holy Spirit. This is not a total definition of evangelism, because it does not include the many possible motives and means involved. There may be various legitimate motives for evangelism. Still, the goal must always be the formation of the biblical Church. This is necessary in order to reach the really ultimate goal of evangelism: the glorification of God.

If new Christian congregations are being formed, then all

other legitimate aims of evangelism are also being reached: Christians are present; they are proclaiming; conversions are taking place; disciples are being made. But if any of these preliminary steps is taken as the primary aim, the biblical growth cycle may be incomplete. Men and women may be genuinely converted and even taught to be disciples, but if they are not formed into the community of God's people, God's plan for the Church as agent of evangelism remains unfulfilled.

Before going into more detail concerning church growth, let us look at the prophetic role of the Church.

**Salt, Light and Sheep among Wolves**     In his life and teachings, Christ showed concretely the values of the Kingdom of God. The Sermon on the Mount tells us what the Kingdom of God is like, the kinds of values and relationships that mark it.

The practical effect and importance of Christ's kingdom teachings have too often been kept in quarantine by two errors. One of these says Christ's words are exclusively for the definitively-established Kingdom and therefore have no application to the contemporary Church in history except as they show what the Kingdom will be (or should have been) like. This kind of dispensationalism must be rejected as unbiblical. It has the same effect as cutting such passages right out of the Bible and rests on a highly selective interpretation. It is the very teachings that strike us as impractical or impossible to apply to which the Church should pay close attention!

The other error says the Sermon on the Mount deals with personal ethics but not with social ethics; therefore the Church must look elsewhere (either to other scriptures or to "the scientific analysis of the class struggle" or to some other teacher) for guidance on social and political questions. This view rests on a false premise and a false dichotomy. The Sermon on the Mount, like Jesus' teachings in general, is highly social if it is anything. There is no dichotomy in Jesus between the individual and the social dimensions. The Christian community is a social fact, and in the Sermon on the Mount Jesus outlines the qualities cherished by that community. "The personhood which he proclaims as a healing, forgiving call to all is integrated into the social novelty of the healing community."[8]

So Jesus shows what the reign of God is like, and the Church's mission is to incarnate and demonstrate the values he taught. The Church is to be a sign of the Kingdom in the world.

Jacques Ellul defines the Christian's function in the world in terms of three figures used by Christ: the salt of the earth, the light of the world and sheep among wolves.[9] Each of these figures suggests a specific function of the Church.

Salt suggests the Church's role of *preservation*. As salt the Church is a sign of the covenant between God and his people (Lev. 2:13). The Church, in covenant relationship with God, leavens society and its structures, preserving them from death and braking the world's mad drive toward self-destruction. It is Christ who moment by moment sustains the fallen creation (Heb. 1:3; Col. 1:17), and at its own level the Church shares in this sustaining work.

As light the Church is a means of *revelation* to men. The Church has no revelation in itself, of course; but it is "a community under the Word." Not only does it live in fidelity to the Word; its function is also to bring the light of the Word to bear on the world and show the true nature of the world's problems. It can do this only because it has first received and obeyed God's Word. Here the Christian's role goes beyond preservation: "He reveals to the world the truth about its condition, and witnesses to the salvation of which it is an instrument."[10]

Finally, the Church lives as sheep among wolves. This suggests the *demonstration* in the flesh of the reality of the

Kingdom. Christ is the Lamb of God, and his little flock, the Church, enters the Kingdom by the same door Jesus had to pass through. Jesus' sacrifice was once and final, but "the life laid down" is the permanent ethical principle for the Church. The only true Christian ethics is crucifixion ethics. Ellul explains:

*In the world everyone wants to be a "wolf," and no one is called to play the part of a "sheep." Yet the world cannot live without this living witness of sacrifice. That is why it is essential that Christians should be very careful not to be "wolves" in the spiritual sense—that is, people who try to dominate others. Christians must accept the domination of other people, and offer the daily sacrifice of their lives, which is united with the sacrifice of Jesus Christ.*[11]

**The Prophetic Role** These comments suggest the basic character of the Church's prophetic role. More specifically, I would outline the following four ways in which the Church fulfills its prophetic function.

1. *The Church is prophetic when it creates and sustains a reconciled and reconciling community of believers* (2 Cor. 5:16-21; Col. 1:21-23; Phil. 2:1-11; Eph. 2:1-22). When this happens, evangelism takes on prophetic dimensions. Reconciliation with God must be demonstrated by genuine reconciliation within the Christian community and by a continuing ministry of reconciliation in the world.

This means that in each local Christian assembly reconciliation must be more than a theory and more than an invisible spiritual transaction. Reconciliation must be real and visible. Racial and economic exploitation and all forms of elitism (including that of a professionalized clergy) must be challenged biblically. Unholy divisions in the body of Christ must be seen as sin and worldliness (1 Cor. 3:3-4). Likewise the local church must work to bring full reconciliation between marriage partners, parents and children, and employer and employee when alienation and discord in these relationships are discovered within the Church (Eph. 5:1—6:9).

Such a community of reconciliation can exist in the world only in active tension with surrounding culture. The differences and distance between the Christian community and the larger human community will vary from one time and place to another, depending on the extent to which culture is godless and under Satan's dominion. As society becomes more godless, the Church must increasingly both see itself and actually structure itself as a self-conscious counterculture. This is necessary for its own faithfulness to the gospel and for any truly prophetic role in the world. In much of the world the Church is moving into an era when it must increasingly take on the marks of a counterculture.

2. *The Church is prophetic when it recognizes and identifies the true enemy* (Mt. 10:28; Lk. 12:4-5; Eph. 6:12; Rom. 8:38-39; 1 Cor. 15:26; Rev. 12:9; 20:2, 14). Satan's trick is to point to false enemies and pose false alternatives. Man in his sin-clouded blindness eagerly follows, for he is only too ready to believe that the real villain is someone else (not himself) and the real power is some impersonal force or historical process (fate, destiny, progress, technology, dialectic—or even "the will of God" in an impersonal, abstract sense). Adam and Eve's reaction in the Garden after their Fall illustrates this moral buck-passing.

Man's true enemy is Satan and the "principalities and powers" under his control (Eph. 6:12 RSV). Therefore true liberation always means first of all breaking the bondage of sin at the personal level through the power of Jesus Christ. "In him we have redemption through his blood, the forgiveness of sins, in accordance with the riches of God's grace" (Eph. 1:7). This means being "made alive" after having been "dead in . . . transgressions and sins" (Eph. 2:1). Salvation begins here; this is the one indispensable narrow gate which Satan wants to block, for it is here that man dies to himself, repudiates Satan and acknowledges God as sovereign and Jesus Christ as the only way to God and thus to God's Kingdom (Acts 4:12).

Satan would introduce a shortcut to the Kingdom that by-passes the cross and gets himself off the hook as the arch-enemy. He perpetually holds out before the Church the same temptation he suggested to Jesus: "All this I will give you . . . if you will bow down and worship me" (Mt. 4:9). Jesus' response is the permanent command for God's people: "Worship the Lord your God, and serve him only" (Mt. 4:10).

The temptation to accept substitute gods and counterfeit satans is always before the Church. At various periods in history the Church has been deceived into warring against false archenemies: Turks, Saracens, insubordination to the hierarchy, rebaptism, the Indians, the Jews, Negroes, whites, Nazism, communism, socialism, the bourgeoisie, capitalism, imperialism. In the name of opposition to these enemies Christians have been willing to put others to death; for when the Church accepts Satan's definition of the enemy, she also readily adopts Satan's tactics.

The Church must see clearly enough both to identify the true enemy and to discern how and where Satan is working today.[12] Satan does work through social structures, ideologies, movements and persons. But the Church must see the enemy behind the enemy in order to avoid false alternatives and a false definition of the problem. She must not reduce faith to ideology—even a religious ideology—and thereby compromise the very gospel itself.

False enemies call forth false solutions which usually are the reverse image of the supposed culprit. Thus the Church is tricked into fighting on the enemy's turf and with his weapons. Too often the Church has let the world define the nature of the battle.

Thus if the foe is seen as communism, Christians are tempted to commit themselves unreservedly to free enterprise. If the enemy is "dependent capitalism and neocolonialism," Christians get behind Marxist socialism. If the danger is a point of doctrine, Christians turn orthodoxy into a bludgeon; if it is a specific behavior, conformity becomes a straitjacket.

The Church must always accept the Bible's definition of man's problem and its identification of the enemy. The Bible is very clear that "the last enemy to be destroyed is death" (1 Cor. 15:26). The identification of this enemy can be a test for the Church. All ideologies, institutions, men and movements are powerless in the face of death. The Church is on target only if its warfare and struggle lead to victory over death. "What sort of savior or god would he be who could not or would not save us from death, sin, and hell?" wrote Martin Luther. "What the true God promises and carries out must be something big."[13] If the Church sees clearly and acts faithfully, it will share Christ's victory over literal, physical death and will also win many kingdom victories along the way. But if it is tricked into fighting false enemies, it will lose its redemptive power and be impotent at the gates of death.

3. *The Church is prophetic when it renounces the world's definition and practice of power* (Mt. 20:20-28; 23:1-12; Mk. 9:35-37; Lk. 9:46-48; 22:24-27; Jn. 13:12-17; Phil. 2:1-11; 1 Cor. 1:18-31). Jesus talked about power, but he insisted that his followers see and use power differently from the way the world does.

The two passages in Matthew (20:20-28; 23:1-12) should be examined carefully. In Matthew 20:25-28, in response to James's and John's request for pre-eminent power in the coming kingdom and in answer to the other disciples' reaction to this request, Jesus said,

*You know that the rulers of the Gentiles lord it over them, and their high officials exercise authority over them. Not so with you. Instead, whoever wants to become great among you must be your servant, and whoever wants to be first must be your slave—just as the Son of Man did not come to be served, but to serve, and to give his life a ransom for many.*

Superficially it appears that the problem here is James's and John's desire for a position not legitimately theirs. But Jesus defines the situation more fundamentally: the world's concept of power must not operate within the Church. "Not so with you." Power in the Church is not a question of position or hierarchy or authority; it is a question of function and of service. The greatness of a Christian is not according to office, status, degrees or reputation, but according to how he or she functions as a servant.

In politics it is different. In politics "high officials exercise authority." But not in the Church. With one statement Jesus rejects the political model for the Church.

Similarly, in Matthew 23:1-12 Jesus rejects the religious hierarchical model. Religious leaders, like political leaders, exercise authority. But they do not practice what they preach. They are concerned about status, position and titles. But what does Jesus say about his own followers?

*You are not to be called "Rabbi," for you have only one Master and you are all brothers. And do not call anyone on earth "father," for you have one Father, and he is in heaven. Nor are you to be called "teacher," for you have one Teacher, the Christ. The greatest among you will be your servant. For whoever exalts himself will be humbled, and whoever humbles himself will be exalted.[14] (Mt. 23:8-12)*

Jesus shows here that the political mindset of Matthew 20: 25 had been assimilated by the established religious leaders. But he rejects it for the Church. Status and authority based on hierarchical position are totally foreign to the kind of community Jesus forms.

It could be argued, of course, that Jesus is merely exhorting to humility here, and not giving a fundamentally different basis of relationships from that of the world. But taken at face value, Jesus' statements in both these passages suggest something more fundamental: the servant or slave is the true model for ministry and relationships among Jesus' followers. And if these teachings were true for the Twelve, they are true for us. They express God's desire for the Christian community in the days between Christ's first and second comings.

What is it that Jesus is rejecting here, really? Is he not rejecting all power based on position and status rather than on Christian character and Christlikeness? This very idea is scandalous to the world for the world says power and position are synonymous and that the goal of power is to control. Jesus says the goal of the Christian is to serve others and glorify God, and the way to such service is through the cross. This is true power, however foolish it appears to the world.

The world is deluded. It believes that real power is a matter of politics. As Jacques Ellul reminds us, "There is a kind of cloud of confusion surrounding politics, a political obsession according to which nothing has significance or importance apart from political intervention and, when all is said and done, all issues are political."[15] This supposed ultimate significance of politics is the "political illusion" to which the Church falls prey. "Therefore we reject all overestimation of political decisions, all idealizing of any political regime. . . ."[16] For politics is relative and by its very nature tends to pose relative questions in absolute terms.

The Church must reject making politics or the State ultimate and sacred. It must renounce political weapons in favor of the armor of God of Ephesians 6:10-20. This passage shows us both the weapons of the Church and, by contrast, those of the world. The stated weapons of the Church are truth, justice, the gospel of peace, faith, salvation, the Word of God and prayer. For each of these the world has its demonic distortion.

In place of truth the world brandishes propaganda. Propaganda is truth twisted for political ends. In secular warfare truth is not sacred but is merely a tool to be used. But in the Church it must not be so! There must be strict adherence to truth in every sense; there can be no compromising here, for God is the God of truth and Jesus Christ is the truth (Jn. 14:6).

In place of justice or righteousness the world substitutes violence and oppresion—and calls them justice. In human warfare righteousness is a victim in almost every sense. The Church must pursue justice defined in biblical terms and must steadfastly reject all violence, manipulation and injustice.

In place of the gospel of peace the world preaches the gospel of power. Liberation becomes a mere power struggle wherein political power is taken from the bad guys and given to the good guys. The weapon of the Church is to preach good news about the *shalom* Christ brings—peace with God, reconciliation among persons and harmony throughout God's creation. The Church renounces the gospel of power as both illusory and ultimately ineffective.

In place of faith the world creates ideology. Ideology is a false faith leading to total commitment to false gods (the Führer, the State or the ideology itself). The world recognizes the value of faith; faith is functional. It is indispensable for warfare. And so faith becomes a technique, merely a means to an end, the tool of ideology. For the Church, "the shield of faith" means total commitment to and dependence on Jesus Christ (not on some "ism" or even "Christianity"). Personal relationship with the living, liberating Jesus is the best defense against ideology.

In place of salvation the world places a false, this-worldly utopia. The world secularizes Christian eschatology and then sacralizes the result. It defines a false Kingdom of God, shaped politically and economically, and then raises this goal to the level of absolute good. But the Church insists on the full biblical meaning of salvation.

In the place of the Word of God the world fabricates its own human sources of revelation. Most often these are science, technology, philosophy or a false messiah (whether political or religious). The Church has no faith in scientific analysis or technological breakthroughs except as these can be shown to be in harmony with the incarnate Word and the written Word. The quickening, discerning Word of God must always be the Church's ultimate source of revelation.

In place of prayer the world substitutes effective action. To the world, prayer is a cop-out and an opiate to keep people from what is really important. But the Church renounces this false view and insists that, in the light of the Word of God, prayer is effective action.

The Church must be marked by total and exclusive reliance on the armor of God. To the world this will appear as weakness and folly. "But God chose the foolish things of the world to shame the wise; and chose the weak things of the world to shame the strong" (1 Cor. 1:27). The gospel and the Church are weak precisely where the world looks for strength. This is the pattern left us by Jesus Christ. Such renunciation of power shows the mystery and the absurdity of the Kingdom of God, and is truly prophetic.

4. *The Church is prophetic when it works for justice in society* (Ps. 82:1-4; Amos 5:21-24; Lk. 3:10-14; 4:18-21; Mt. 11:4-6; Eph. 5:11). Christians bear a particular responsibility to the poor and oppressed. God's people are called to defend the cause of the poor and needy within each nation and worldwide.[17] The treatment of the poor, the needy and "those who have no social power"[18] becomes a test of the justness of any society or political system. Therefore when the Church works in behalf of the poor it is meeting specific human need and it is making a politically significant contribution.

The Church works for the physical and social needs of people not as though this were the primary or exclusive task of the Church but as a testimony that redemption and holiness (which are truly spiritual and moral) include every area of life.

In the political sphere the Church is concerned less about equality than about liberty and the safeguarding of personal rights and dignities, especially those of the defenseless. The gospel is first of all a message of liberation, and then, derivatively, of equality. An insistence on liberty is necessary to guarantee that any achieved equality not degenerate into a lowest-common-denominator equalism understood in merely quantitative or economic terms.

Whether and how Christians should participate in political processes is a many-sided question that depends upon a multitude of factors. Perhaps we can conceive of a continuum, at one end of which is *counterculture* and at the other, *political and social participation.* In some contexts the Church must exist almost exclusively as a counterculture; in other situations society may be so leavened by the gospel that active political and social participation is possible. Between these two poles lies a broad range of likely roles for the Church. In any specific context, as culture deteriorates morally and spiritually and comes increasingly under Satan's domination, the Church must move progressively from active involvement to the counterculture stance. Presumably movement in the other direction would be possible under opposite conditions. These issues and circumstances require great spiritual discernment.

The Church is prophetic when it is truly the messianic community which reveals the nature of the Kingdom and the mind and stature of Jesus Christ. As it carries on the works of Christ it fulfills its kingdom tasks.

But this will never be a neat, clear-cut, triumphant road for the Church to follow. Obedience to the gospel in a world where Satan is still active means living with tension. This is part of the meaning of the Incarnation. The Incarnation makes sense only through faith in God. If it is faithful, the Church's career will largely parallel that of Jesus Christ.

We, as Christians, can never be sure we have all the answers or see all things clearly or are really "making progress." We are therefore constantly forced back to total dependence on the incarnate Christ. We should be alarmed when we are at home in the world or have total "peace of mind." Christian life in a non-Christian world is tension, stress and at times even agony. A whole system of social techniques aims to adjust the individual to the world and eliminate tensions. But being a Jesus-follower means accepting the scandal of Jesus' statements that he came to bring not harmony but discord; not peace but a sword (Mt. 10:34-36). For only thus may true peace finally come.

In summary, the Church's kingdom tasks include the proclamation of the gospel in such a way that men and women respond in faith and obedience to Jesus and join in building the Christian community. This community is a new social reality which, through its likeness to Christ and its renunciation of the world's definitions and tactics, reveals the true nature of God's reign. "Our Lord called and continues to call out a new society of persons unconditionally committed to exchanging the values of the surrounding society for the standards of Jesus' kingdom."[19] Only on this basis can the Church work with integrity for justice and peace in the world. Thus the prophetic and evangelistic dimensions of the gospel are totally interwoven in the life and witness of the community of the King.

It may be helpful to backtrack a bit and explore a question raised earlier: What is the relationship between church growth and the Kingdom of God?

# 7

## CHURCH GROWTH
## AND KINGDOM GROWTH

Is growth of the Church the same as the progress of the Kingdom of God? Does numerical church growth contribute to kingdom growth?

Church growth does advance the Kingdom of God—provided that by *church growth* one means the growth, both numerical and spiritual, of the genuine community of God's people. In Scripture God's plan through the Church is joined with his purpose to "reconcile all things" in Jesus Christ. Jesus is both head of creation and head of the Church (Eph. 1:10, 22-23; Col. 1:17-20). The mission of the Church is to demonstrate this headship within the Christian fellowship and to show signs of its truth in all areas of life. The Church's task is to live out its faith that Christ has in fact conquered the principalities and powers, and thus to work for the progressive manifestation of the Kingdom until Jesus Christ returns to earth to establish finally and eternally the reign of God.

The same God who reigns over the world is the God of the Church, the Father of Jesus Christ. When faithful to the gospel, therefore, the Church through its growth furthers the cause of the Kingdom. But a word of warning! If we confuse institutional church structures with the authentic Church of Jesus Christ, we may be deceived into equating institutional church success with kingdom growth. This is a lie and a deception and leads to idolatry. The numerical growth of a denomination does not further the Kingdom of God unless that denomination is faithful to the gospel in its internal community life, its worship and its witness in the world. The letters to the seven churches in Revelation should stand before us as a constant warning.

But God has called his Church to make disciples of all peoples throughout all lands and this implies numerical growth. Disciples are countable. Thus we have the startling and yet very matter-of-fact recording of numerical growth in the book of Acts. Luke gives us enough statistics to show that when the Spirit acts the Church grows numerically, but not enough to allow us to seize on numerical growth as the essence of the Church or as the only measure of a church's life and effectiveness. It is crucial to maintain a biblical balance here.

How does the Church grow, and how does the Kingdom grow? We will examine in some detail the process of church growth and then compare this with kingdom growth.

**Normal Church Growth**   The community of God's people grows by bringing people to faith in Jesus Christ and incorporating these new disciples into the body of believers. This should be the normal pattern of church growth. Several aspects of this growth process need to be discussed.

Normal church growth means growth which conforms to the norm of the gospel. By *normal* I mean neither average nor customary. Rather, I mean the growth which follows when the Church adheres to the biblical norm for its life, structure and witness. This is the only norm which counts, and the only valid criterion.

There is something spontaneous about genuine church growth. Normal growth does not depend upon successful techniques or programs, although planning has its place. Rather, growth is the normal consequence of spiritual life.

What is alive grows. Normal church growth is spontaneous in the sense that the nature of the Church is to grow—spiritually, numerically and in its cultural impact. Like Jesus, its growth should be "in wisdom and stature, and in favor with God and men" (Lk. 2:52). Roland Allen was right to speak of "the spontaneous expansion of the Church."[1]

Church growth is not a matter of bringing to the Church that which is necessary for growth, for if Christ is there, the seeds of growth are already present. Rather, church growth is a matter of removing the hindrances to growth. The Church will naturally grow if not limited by unbiblical barriers.

What are some of these barriers? Potentially they are many: spiritual disunity, immorality and false doctrine are some that come to mind from the New Testament church. Two other hindrances which relate especially to the nature and structure of the Church are unbiblical traditions and rigid institutional structures. These were two of the factors found in Judaism which necessitated the formation of a church distinct from Judaism when Christ came. Speaking to the scribes and Pharisees Jesus said, "You nullify the word of God for the sake of your tradition" (Mt. 15:6). On another occasion he said, "New wine must be poured into new wineskins" (Lk. 5:38). On both occasions he was referring to the traditions and structures which had grown up in Judaism and were actually stifling God's work.

The same thing has happened countless times in church history. Unbiblical traditions and structures have limited the growth of the Church until they either were corrected or (more often) burst open as new wine bursts old wineskins.

Of course, these barriers result from sin as do immorality and false doctrine, but more in the sense of our failure, due to the Fall, to perceive and faithfully follow God's plan for the Church. I have already called attention to the clergy-laity dichotomy which tends to limit growth by stifling "lay" initiative and the exercise of gifts essential for growth. Other factors are the institutional church's edifice complex or dependence on buildings, the rigidity of denominational and missionary structures, and inflexible traditions as to time and form of church gatherings.[2] Sterile worship patterns are a particular problem and a crucial area where reform is needed.[3]

Normal church growth occurs especially among the poorer masses. Michael Green notes that the early Christians "appealed to the simple, unlettered lower classes for the most part," and "such continued to be the general trend for some time to come, though with notable exceptions."[4] Tertullian said in the second century, "The uneducated are always a majority with us." From the beginning and throughout history, the most rapid, enduring and society-transforming church growth has normally occurred among the poor.[5]

We face here, however, not merely an empirical fact but also a biblical mandate. Both the example and teachings of Jesus Christ bear out his statement that, in fulfillment of prophecy, he had come "to preach good news to the poor" (Lk. 4:18).

Normal church growth is not really limited by lack of financial resources or physical facilities. We do not find Paul complaining that more could be accomplished if only more funds were available. Nor is there any evidence that the early church was hindered in its growth by its lack of church buildings. If anything, the opposite is true. Heavy financial investment in buildings, property and programs intended to facilitate church growth often becomes instead a limiting factor. Emphasis is shifted to these things and the vision for ministering the gospel simply and directly to persons is dimmed or lost altogether.

The history of missions bears this out. In Brazil, for instance, there is a pronounced inverse correlation between church growth and the amount of funds received from outside the country. Those denominations which receive the most help financially grow most slowly; those receiving little monetary assistance grow rapidly.

Obviously other factors may be involved here (wise stewardship, the extent and maturity of indigenous leadership, the strength and length of strings attached). And unquestionably Christian love and stewardship will demand the sharing of resources across cultures. Yet the fact remains that rapid church growth does not depend upon either money or buildings. It is more likely to depend on the availability of people—either foreign or national—who are ready to exercise their gifts in witness and ministry.

This is not to argue against the disciplined investment of funds and buildings in specific ministries such as schools, hospitals, orphanages and so forth. These auxiliary, supportive institutions may well serve the overall interests of the Kingdom. But neither they nor other forms of major financial involvement are the key to normal church growth.

**Church-Growth Life Cycle** There is a pattern to church growth. Growth varies from place to place and from time to time; yet certain patterns emerge consistently.

The Holy Spirit produces church growth; it is he who draws people to Christ. Looking at the New Testament and church history, we can perceive some of the ways the Spirit works in producing such growth. I wish to emphasize in particular four factors which are essential components of growth and which are grounded in the basic biblical nature of the Church. Donald McGavran and others have rightly pointed out the importance of external factors—political, religious, ideological, socioeconomic and other influences—which determine the receptivity of a people. These also need to be taken into consideration but do not relate directly to the nature of the Church itself.

These four factors constitute the life cycle of the Church as it grows and reproduces itself. They are (1) telling the good news, (2) multiplying congregations, (3) building Christian community and (4) exercising spiritual gifts.

1. *Telling the good news.* The mandate for proclamation is central in God's cosmic plan, for this plan centers in what God is doing for people. It concerns the redemption that brings eternal salvation and builds the Church.

The Church after Pentecost evangelized irrepressibly. The great concern and dynamic of the early church was to tell the good news about Jesus and the resurrection, bearing witness to what they had seen, heard and experienced. The evangelistic impulse is inherent in the gospel and in the experience of conversion and Spirit baptism.

The evangelistic task of the Church is to proclaim the good news of salvation in Jesus Christ throughout the world, making disciples and building the Church (Mt. 28:19-20; Mk. 16: 15). Therefore evangelism must always be the first priority of the Church's ministry in the world.

2. *Multiplying Christian congregations.* Evangelistic proclamation is not an end in itself, however. It must lead beyond itself to making disciples. Not mere numerical growth but the multiplication of local churches is the test of a healthy, growing church. The biblical ideal is neither to produce a host of new Christians who live unattached, separated lives, nor to expand existing local churches until their membership bulges into the thousands. The biblical pattern is to form new converts into local congregations and to multiply the number of congregations as new converts are added.

The ministry of Paul and other New Testament evangelists was a church-multiplying ministry. Converts in many cities quickly ran into the thousands; yet for nearly two hundred years no church buildings were erected. Such growth under such conditions can be explained only as the multiplication of small congregations. It is not surprising, therefore, that the New Testament often refers to "the church in your [or their] house"[6] (Rom. 16:5; 1 Cor. 16:19; Col. 4:15; Philem. 2).

A pastor said recently, "I am convinced that the local church can become a great institution." That's true, but it is the wrong focus. There is too easy a tendency to build large local churches with the accompanying inevitable institutionalism, bureaucracy and emphasis on buildings. The subtle temptation to imitate secular institutional models such as government, industry and the university becomes overwhelming, and the church slips into institutionalism with the rigidity, impersonality and hierarchy that go along with the package.

Normal growth comes by the division of cells, not by the unlimited expansion of existing cells. The growth of individual cells beyond a certain point without division is pathological. Church-growth studies verify that "only as the number of churches is multiplied does the Christian part of the overall population increase" in a given society.[7]

The optimum size of a local congregation will vary of course according to cultural factors, and no arbitrary limit can be set. Church-growth research would seem to suggest, however, that once a congregation has grown to a few hundred members the rate of growth will slow down unless new branch congregations are formed through growth by division. Where notable exceptions to this pattern are found, closer examination will usually reveal that the local "congregation" running into the thousands is in reality a whole network of smaller "subcongregations" in which growth by division is taking place as the normal pattern.[8]

Growth comes by the multiplication of congregations of believers, not necessarily by the multiplication of church buildings or institutional structures. If the Church can grow only as fast as buildings are built or pastors are academically trained or budgets are expanded, then growth is limited to the resources available for these purposes. The early church was strikingly unlimited by such factors. And these are not the real hindrances to church growth today.

3. *Building Christian community.* Even the multiplication of Christian congregations is not the final goal, however. Multiplication must lead to the edification of the Christian community in each particular case, for God's will is that "all reach unity in the faith and in the knowledge of the Son of God" (Eph. 4:13). This is discipleship.

Evangelism requires the existence of a witnessing community if church growth is to become a continuing process. As suggested in chapter five, effective proclamation presupposes the existence of a community of believers who do the proclaiming. This is true even in the most pagan society where no organized church yet exists. For even there, as soon as Christian witnesses enter the society the Church is present (Mt. 18: 20), and hearers are called to join the new community. While one can, of course, point to some exceptions, this seems to be the normal biblical pattern.

Neither Jesus, Peter nor Paul normally evangelized alone. Almost immediately after his baptism, Jesus had disciples around him—an incipient Christian community (Jn. 1:29-42). Jesus sent his disciples out two by two, not one by one. Peter took others with him to Samaria and to Cornelius's house in Caesarea (Acts 8:14; 10:23). Paul was nearly always accompanied by one or more companions; Acts 13:13 speaks of "Paul and his company" (RSV) or "Paul and his companions" (NIV). Although there are exceptions to this pattern (Philip in Acts 8:4-8 and 8:26-40; Paul in Athens), they do seem to be exceptions, not the rule.[9] Normally, where the missionaries went the Church went with them (in the sense of at least one companion), so that the evangelistic call was a call, in part, to an already-existing and demonstrated communal fellowship, a new way of living together. This gives new meaning to Jesus' statement about being present in the midst of two or three gathered believers (Mt. 18:20), as well as to household evangelism.

Many churches do not share the gospel effectively because

their communal experience of the gospel is too weak and
tasteless to be worth sharing. It does not excite the believer to
the point where he wants to witness, and (as the believer un-
comfortably suspects) it is not all that attractive to the un-
believer. But where Christian fellowship demonstrates the
gospel, believers come alive and sinners get curious and want
to know what the secret is. So true Christian community
(*koinonia*) becomes both the basis and the goal of evangelism.

One of the important functions of Christian community
life is the maintenance of discipline and accepted group standards. Here community and doctrine come together and
"orthodoxy of belief" is joined to "orthodoxy of community,"
to use Francis Schaeffer's terms. The community is the only
effective school for discipleship.[10] For all these reasons, building true *koinonia* is an indispensable link in the life cycle of
church growth.

4. *Exercising spiritual gifts.* The importance of spiritual gifts
in relation to community has already been stressed in chapter
five. Here I emphasize that the awakening and exercise of
gifts is an essential part of the process of church growth. A
truly charismatic church is a growing church. Growth produces diversity, and diversity brings more growth. That's the
secret of the Church, the gift-bearing body.

We should not think, therefore, that only the gift of evangelism is evangelistic! All spiritual gifts contribute to evangelism in one way or another. In the first place, several of the
God-appointed leaders (those gifted as apostles, prophets and
evangelists especially) carry out significant evangelistic work
in the world. This evangelism serves to win converts,
strengthen and train the Church in its own day-by-day evangelism and witness, and to interpret to the world the source
of the Church's life. Second, individual believers have an
evangelistic witness in the world as they are equipped to do so
by the equipping ministers. Though every person will not be
a gifted evangelist, the faithful exercise of each gift will be a

true witness to the love of Christ. Third, those who exercise the more "inward" gifts of healing, encouragement, teaching and so forth, provide the continuing spiritual support (and sometimes even economic support) for those who carry on evangelism in the world. Fourth, those who exercise their gifts to sustain the inward life of the community contribute to evangelism through training and integrating new converts into the Church—an essential and oft-neglected function. Finally, this harmonious overall functioning of the Christian fellowship is a demonstration of the truth of the gospel and thus is a witness in and to the world.

As we examine these four components of growth, we see that they are not isolated factors but that each contributes to the others in an ongoing cycle of edification and expansion (Figure 3). When the Church is growing biblically, gospel proclamation leads to the multiplication of congregations. This provides the Church's major evangelistic impact in the world as new churches are formed. Within each congrega-

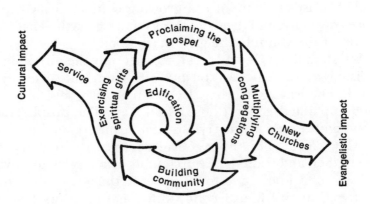

**Figure 3.** Life Cycle of the Local Church

tion, however, true Christian community must be built. As the community "builds itself up in love," a kaleidoscope of spiritual gifts is awakened and begins to function, and discipleship is taken seriously. Through their gifts, believers minister outwardly to the world and inwardly to the Christian community.

One result is substantial healing in the various areas of society; this produces a significant cultural impact glorifying to God. Some gifts are more directly evangelistic and thus strengthen and continue the Church's evangelistic thrust; and so the dynamic cycle of normal church growth is completed.

This cycle is what happens on the horizontal plane, as it were. Such growth is truly biblical, however, only as the Church maintains a living and vital relationship vertically with God. Thus a more complete conception of the Church's life is suggested by Figure 4. A careful evaluation of each of the elements of this diagram should reveal the weak links in the life

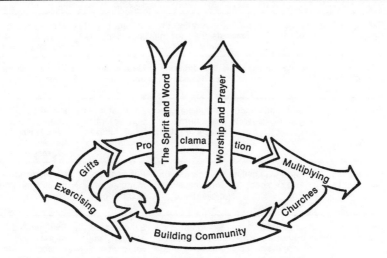

**Figure 4.** Normal Church Life

cycle of any church or evangelistic organization. (Some further aspects of this fourfold analysis of church growth are suggested in Table 2.)

**Growth by Division**    Growth by division, or the multiplication of local congregations, is not a biblical principle in the same sense that Christian community life or the exercise of spiritual gifts are biblical principles. It is rather a conclusion

| | Evangelistic Proclamation | Multiplying Congregations | Building Community | Exercising Gifts |
|---|---|---|---|---|
| Words of Christ | Go into all the world and preach the good news (Mk. 16:15). You will be my witnesses (Acts 1:8). | Make disciples of all nations (Mt. 28:19). Jerusalem . . . Judea and Samaria and to the end of the earth (Acts 1:8) | Teaching them to obey everything I have commanded you (Mt. 28:19). That they may be one as we are one (Jn. 17:22). | If a man remains in me . . . will bear much fruit (Jn. 15:5). He will do even greater things than these (Jn. 14:12). |
| Example of Christ | Proclamation of the good news | Preparation of disciples for this ministry | Community life with disciples | Jesus' preaching, healing, counseling, teaching, etc. |
| Life Principle | Seed planting | Reproduction, cell division | Metabolism, body life | Vine and branch, diversity within unity |
| Function | Communication, gaining converts | Establishing new churches, conserving fruit, follow-up | Spiritual maturation, equipping, "perfecting," discipline | Ministry inward and outward, evangelism, fulfillment, self-expression |
| Related Movements | Mass evangelism and personal evangelism movements | Church growth, some missionary movements | Renewal movement, small-group movements | Charismatic movement, Pentecostalism |
| Dangers of Partial Emphasis | Lost fruit, spiritual starvation, evangelistic technology | Exaggerated denominationalism, success mentality, accommodation to the world | Exaggerated subjectivism, self-centeredness, withdrawal from world | Exaggerated individualism, neglect of doctrine, factiousness |

**Table 2. Four Factors in Normal Church Growth**

many have reached through studying the New Testament church and church growth throughout history. Its biblical basis is twofold: the analogy from physical life and the example of the early church.

It will be helpful at this point to answer several questions that have been raised concerning the principle of growth by division in the life cycle of the Church.

*Is growth by division possible in all situations?* The multiplication of local cells of believers is more difficult in some cultures than in others, but it is totally impossible only under the most repressive totalitarian regimes. Where the vigilance of the State is practically complete, this principle will be difficult to follow. This is something we must leave in the hands of God.

It is important to point out, however, that I am speaking here neither of the multiplication of buildings nor of the multiplication of official government-sanctioned church organizations. I am speaking of the proliferation of local, perhaps highly informal, cells of Christian believers. In totalitarian regimes these may not be able to grow into large organized churches, but the multiplication of small fellowships is often possible, even if risky. In some cases, however, the Church must simply continue to live as the suffering Church, its community life restricted almost totally to individual families, awaiting either the day of harvest or the day of deliverance. Recent reports from mainland China reveal a widespread underground proliferation of local Christian cells which suggests that such growth is possible under totalitarian government. In this case, in fact, it is the only kind of church growth which is possible! In the majority of cases growth by division can take place if there is the vision for it.

*Is growth by division wise in areas where many Christian churches already exist?* In some areas where the Church has been established for centuries, too many churches appear to exist, even though many of these are only nominally Christian. Is multiplication really the answer in such cases?

Again, I am not speaking of multiplying buildings or organizations. In many Western cities, the last thing the Church needs is more buildings! What it often does need, however, is to rediscover true Christian community or fellowship. The small group is helpful here. And as small groups are formed, they will tend to multiply. The number of official organized churches may remain the same while the number of biblical churches is actually multiplying rapidly as more and more individuals discover new life in Christ and new lifestyle in true Christian community. This was the pattern of the sixteenth-century Reformation, both in its mainstream and radical forms. Rather than discouraging such a movement, the organized churches should encourage and stimulate it, and seek to guide it in biblical channels.

*Does not division usually occur for carnal rather than spiritual reasons?* Too often this is the case. Many churches have multiplied and grown, not because they had a vision for growth but simply because the brethren could not get along with each other! This is clearly wrong, and yet God has miraculously used such divisions for the growth of the Church.

But unholy splits often develop precisely because of the lack of a healthy vision for church multiplication. If new churches are formed with the vision for eventual growth by division, if this is understood from the beginning, then growth will occur naturally for the right rather than the wrong reasons.

Churches may divide for wrong motives, but this fact does not cancel out the multiplication principle, any more than cancer invalidates the principle of normal cell division. Multiplication growth may be planned for the right reasons, rather than letting it occur for the wrong reasons.

*Doesn't the multiplication of small groups and church communities increase the potential for going astray doctrinally?* Multiplication does increase the risk, for more life means more chance for aberrations. But there are safeguards. The most potent of these are the Spirit and the Word. The first must be carefully heeded; the second, carefully studied and applied throughout the Church. Also, it is important within a local church or cluster of churches to have some coordination of efforts for church multiplication. Fearful local church leaders sometimes fail to realize that a ministry of small groups and cell multiplication, started and coordinated by the local church, is much more likely to stay on the track doctrinally than groups which form independently when the church fails to provide this kind of leadership. It makes more sense to provide needed food than to condemn alien sources of supply.

*Where does the Church find sufficient leadership when new congregations are formed?* The answer to this question is found in discipleship, spiritual gifts and the community life of the Church. If we live with our brothers and sisters in true Christian community and if we expect the Spirit to provide the necessary spiritual gifts, the right gifts of leadership will appear at the right time to take care of the demands of growth. Traditional church structure, with its low ratio of leaders to followers, often fails to develop latent leadership because responsibilities are concentrated in a few people.

When we find persons who are gifted as church multipliers we can work with them and guide them toward increased effectiveness. Normally growth by division should be a charismatic process based on spiritual gifts.

The multiplication of congregations should result from the growth of small-group fellowships. Such groups offer the ideal structure to awaken, discipline and train spiritual gifts. Growth by division is simply one step in the overall process of the Church's life and growth. When the Church is truly the community of God's people, it is God the Spirit who provides the necessary leadership. This is his promise to us.

*Doesn't growth by division weaken the mother church?* Where growth by division is part of an ongoing process, as outlined above, it strengthens rather than weakens the mother church. A continuing, expected exodus from the mother church creates new opportunities for community and the use of spiritual gifts among those who remain. Unused or undetected gifts and ministries emerge. A local church should measure its success not by buildings or budgets but by the number of spiritual children and grandchildren it has produced. This is especially true of larger churches. Churches may only be getting fatter, not healthier. To give birth to a new congregation is one of the highest privileges granted to a local church, and is a hundred times more significant than large budgets, multiple staff and new buildings.

The mother church will not suffer, provided it is itself living and growing on biblical principles. If it is structured according to a charismatic rather than an institutional model, it will flourish. But if it is institutionally structured and depends heavily on a long roster of boards and committees, it will have difficulty producing new congregations. As I have already suggested, growth by division is an organic and charismatic process, not an institutional one.[11]

**A Plant and Yeast** The Kingdom of God—not just the Church—is intended to grow. In fact, Jesus spoke more about kingdom growth than about church growth! He spoke of the progressive extension of God's reign over nations and peoples until the promised Kingdom has fully arrived (Mt. 13:18-52; Mk. 4:26-32; Lk. 13:18-20). Scripture reveals God's plan to bring all creation under the headship of Jesus Christ. God spoke to the nations long ago through Isaiah, saying:

*Turn to me and be saved,*
*all the ends of the earth!*
*For I am God, and there is no other.*
*By myself I have sworn,*
*from my mouth has gone forth in righteousness*
*a word that shall not return:*

*"To me every knee shall bow,*
*every tongue shall swear." (Is. 45:22-23)*

Paul picked up the same theme, saying, "At the name of Jesus every knee should bow, in heaven and on earth and under the earth, and every tongue confess that Jesus Christ is Lord, to the glory of God the Father" (Phil. 2:10-11). There is a progressive, hidden growth of the Kingdom of God, even in the face of severe satanic fury and opposition, until Christ returns to definitively establish his reign.

*Then the end will come, when he hands over the kingdom to God the Father after he has destroyed all dominion, authority and power. For he must reign until God has put all his enemies under his feet. The last enemy to be destroyed is death. For God "has put everything under his feet." . . . When he has done this, then the Son himself will be made subject to him who put everything under him, so that God may be all in all. (1 Cor. 15:24-28)*

The growth of the Kingdom of God is the progressive extension of God's reign over all creation. It is not a geographic growth. The central battleground in the struggle between God's Kingdom and Satan's counterfeit is people's minds and hearts. It is here that the clash of wills takes place: "The kingdom of God is within you" (Lk. 17:21).

Jesus frequently spoke of the Kingdom of God as a hidden reality which people may now enter or experience but which will become manifest only in the future. To the eyes of the world the Kingdom is absent or dormant, but believers know that in Jesus the Kingdom has drawn near (Mt. 4:17; 10:7) and is in their midst (Lk. 17:21). The Kingdom can and must be preached and proclaimed (Mt. 24:14; Lk. 4:43; 8:1; 9:2, 60; 10:9-11). Now its presence is a secret seen only by the eyes of faith. But that does not mean the Kingdom is now absent, or that it is static or frozen. It continues to spread and grow, but in a hidden way.

Something strange and wonderful is happening in the world, and the world does not know what it is. And it won't believe because it sees no great power—no armies or parliaments to impress it. But Christians know the Kingdom of God has appeared in Jesus, is now present implicitly in the Church, is at work secretly in the world and will come in true, creative, restoring and judging power when Jesus Christ returns to earth.

Several of Jesus' parables speak of the growth of the Kingdom. We note especially the two parables recorded in Matthew 13:31-33.

*The kingdom of heaven is like a mustard seed, which a man took and planted in his field. Though it is the smallest of all your seeds, yet when it grows, it is the largest of garden plants and becomes a tree, so that the birds of the air come and perch in its branches. . . . The kingdom of heaven is like yeast that a woman took and mixed into a large amount of flour until it worked all through the dough.*

A plant and yeast. These are analogies from life. The same God who hid life in the mustard seed and in the yeast cell is daily working imperceptibly to reconcile all things in Jesus Christ. That's how the Kingdom grows. The beginnings are small and unimpressive, but growth comes and the Kingdom advances.

So kingdom growth is not the same as church growth. The two are related; the same God is at work; it is the same Jesus who is Lord. But the growth of the Kingdom is more hidden, more mysterious, more subtle. Church growth is visible and can be studied statistically; the growth of the Kingdom can never be equated with quantitative church growth. The growth of the Kingdom can never be manipulated by human techniques; it is always, invariably, true to the very nature of the King. It operates only and exclusively on the basis of the pattern of truth and life revealed in Jesus Christ.

The Kingdom of God is the kingdom of truth. It knows no falsehood, no lie. How does the Kingdom grow? Like yeast; like leaven. So where the gospel has gone in fidelity, there truth has leavened society. The Church may be very small numerically, yet the power of truth works its way into the fabric of society, winnowing out falsehood. It is largely the fruit of the gospel that in many cultures today social and caste barriers have fallen, slavery is seen as wrong and inhuman, and pagan religions have been cleansed of their grosser elements. Communism itself is a product of Christian truth in the sense that it has taken certain Christian ideals (fraternity, classless society, peace), secularized them, and made them the basis of a false and demonic kingdom vision.

So the Kingdom of God works like yeast. It leavens cultures and social systems, replacing the false with the true. Yet Satan is at work to subvert truth wherever found, twist it and turn it against God.

The Church must always witness to the reign of God. It must never be satisfied with its own numerical growth and lose sight of its true goal. It must remember that it is the community of the King, and never become indifferent to the quality and integrity of the gospel it proclaims and demonstrates. It must provide the base for just and truly reconciled human society, especially in Third World countries where growing nationalism, the inherent idealism of youth, and new emerging political and economic influence must be reckoned with. It is crucial that the whole gospel be preached and lived out in all its prophetic as well as evangelistic dimensions. We must take care precisely at this point if we are concerned about the witness and fidelity of the Church not just today but fifty and one hundred years from now.

In the previous chapter we examined the prophetic role of the Christian community. When the Church is truly prophetic, it advances the cause of the Kingdom. And when it is both prophetic and evangelistic, it is true to the Kingdom. Then church growth means kingdom growth.

# 8
## THE FORM
## OF THE CHURCH

Once upon a time there was a man named Bill who was fed up with the institutional church. "The Church is so locked in to tradition," he said, "that no spiritual freedom can exist. It's hopeless! I give up on the institutional church."

So Bill gathered a small group of like-minded friends together. "We're going to throw out all the institutionalism and have a simple, unstructured, New Testament church," said Bill.

They all got together one Sunday evening. Eleven of them. They spent about two and one-half hours just sharing, singing, praying and studying the Bible. It was great! Everyone was excited. This was the first time most of them had experienced such free, open fellowship, and the group felt drawn together and spiritually strengthened.

As it came time to break up that evening, Bill said, "Well, this has really been great! I think we've got something started here. Can we meet again next week?"

Everyone agreed. Same time, same place. (The practical question of space and time again.) This new experience of fellowship was worth continuing.

And so a new fellowship—in effect, a new local church—was born. The group grew, diversified somewhat and met various needs as they arose. What about child care? What about time and length of meetings? What about leadership? What about special holiday observances? What about the cost of materials? In each case, ongoing, fixed arrangements were worked out so the group could function smoothly and would not have to keep making the same minor decisions all over again.

It worked. The group prospered.

But was it unstructured? Of course not! It immediately developed its own structures; it inevitably took on institutional form. Perhaps the forms adopted were good forms; perhaps they were much better than those which had been left behind and better served the true purpose of the Church. Probably so. But structures did indeed appear, for all life must have form. Life without form is sick and dies; it perishes because it cannot sustain itself. That's the way it is with all life, whether spiritual, human or botanical, for God in his creation is consistent.

So we come now to the question of church structure, the form of the Church. The thesis of this chapter is that structure is inevitable, but that not all church structures are equally valid.

We have seen what the Church is biblically: the community of God's people, not an institutional or organizational structure. We also have seen how the Church accomplishes God's plan: through demonstrating the reality of God's salvation in community, and by performing those preordained works which bring substantial healing and point toward the future definitive establishing of the Kingdom of God. Further, we have seen that the Church carries out its mandate by being the messianic community and by witnessing according to the gifts God gives. This is what it means to be the community of the King.

As we take a closer look at structure, I emphasize that the structure is not the Church, just as the wineskin is not the wine. But the structure is necessary in order for the Church to live and serve in space and time. Every Christian fellowship must have a culturally appropriate way of doing things at certain times and in certain places.

A church which intends to grow and serve the Kingdom of God must be structured in harmony with the biblical understanding of the Church. This is not to say that a church structured otherwise will not grow, for churches with the most diverse structures have obviously grown and survived. But a church not structured in harmony with biblical principles will never achieve the quality of growth and the authenticity of discipleship which God intends.

In itself, church structure is neither evil nor illegitimate. The question concerns the kinds of structures which best serve the Church in its life and witness. Particular structures will be legitimate or illegitimate depending not only on what they are intended to accomplish, but on their function—what they actually do accomplish.

This chapter will look first at criteria for workable structures: How can we be sure specific wineskins are really functional? Second, we will look at the need for structures which especially aid the Church in its witness, and distinguish between the Church and para-church structures. Finally, we will suggest some possible guidelines for church structure today and apply these to the question of the Church's cross-cultural witness.

**Workable Structures** The Bible gives very little specific guidance regarding church structure. It paints a clear profile of what the Church is intended to be, and gives the early history of the Church in two cultural contexts: Palestinian Jewish society and first-century Greco-Roman society. On the basis of this biblical witness the Church in every age forms those wineskins which seem most compatible with its nature and mission within its cultural context.

The question of structure arises within the broad area of freedom within form which the Bible allows. Specific structures are not explicitly prescribed in Scripture. Yet the biblical picture of the Church does help us outline practical criteria for evaluating church structure in any historical context. I suggest three. (It will be helpful to recall here the discussion in chapter four concerning the institutional versus charismatic model for understanding the Church.)

First, *church structure must be biblically valid.* That is, church structure must be compatible with the nature and form of the gospel and of the Church as biblically presented.

New Testament writers were zealous to guard the truth of the gospel and the Church against encroachments from the world or from Judaism. To insist on circumcision was to deny the gospel (Gal. 5:2-6). To make distinctions within the Christian community on the basis of wealth, social status or religious traditions was to transgress God's law (Jas. 2:1-13; Gal. 2:11-21). Jesus warned against canceling out the Word of God by adhering to human tradition (Mt. 15:6). Any tradition, structure or pattern which leads believers to contradict in practice what they profess in faith is unbiblical and must be rejected.

Although this principle should be obvious and fundamental, it is frequently violated. Structures are formed or spawned which are basically contrary to the Bible. They become the unbiblical traditions and rigid institutions mentioned earlier. Yet how often in the Church—even at the local level—we fracture the fellowship into rich and poor, ministers and laymen, black and white, young and old. How devoted we become to preserving programs and how little devoted we are to each other or to structures which help us truly be the Church. We need to ask some hard (and, to some people, shocking) questions: Is the traditional Sunday school structure biblically defensible? Do believers really worship or encounter God in our church services? Is the Word of God really taught and heard? Do believers really "speak the truth in love" to one another, or only say nice, meaningless things? Do our structures take seriously the gifts of the Spirit and the priesthood of believers? Are there viable structures for *koinonia* and for mission?

Quite simply, the criterion of biblical validity means that all church structures should in fact help the Church be the Church and carry out its mission. They should be structures which promote community, build disciples and sustain witness. Structures which in fact do this are valid; structures which do not are invalid, regardless of how esthetic, efficient or venerated they may be.

Second, *church structure must be culturally viable*. It must be compatible with the cultural forms of the society in which the Church finds itself. This means that church structures cannot be uncritically transplanted from one culture to another without causing serious problems and fundamental misunderstandings as to the true nature of the Church.

The first-century church, for all its problems, still provides remarkable examples of cultural adaptation and viability. Through Stephen, Philip, Paul and others, the early church quickly reached into the Greek-speaking Mediterranean world (Acts 6 and following). Meeting in homes, and generally following the synagogue pattern in local structure, the first Christians were able to multiply rapidly without a large organizational superstructure. Through a pattern of itinerant preachers and evangelists the church maintained a network of communication, teaching and church planting which reached throughout much of the Roman Empire. This pattern was used with great effect by the mendicant preaching orders in the later Middle Ages.

In the modern missionary age, the Church has grown most effectively and most authentically when it has been able to adapt to cultural realities without compromising the transcultural truth of the gospel. On the other hand, the violation of the principle of cultural viability has at times resulted in slow penetration where cultural differences were great. One of the main factors behind slow church growth in Japan has been the introduction of traditions concerning congregational life and the pastoral ministry which were foreign and not culturally appropriate. This is a violation of the principle of cultural viability. (One may question as well whether these traditions were biblically valid.)

But one need not cross the ocean to encounter a different culture. Modern cities are a cultural microcosm, so effective ministry in urban areas demands sensitivity at this point.

Obviously, biblical validity takes precedence over cultural viability. The Church, after all, will always be in tension with the surrounding culture. But we must take pains to make sure that this tension comes from the antithesis between light and darkness, not from the incompatibility of cultural forms. Where possible, the Church should structure itself along the lines of other structures of a given culture. But this calls for discernment, as it can be done only to the extent that biblical faithfulness is not compromised.

The Church cannot uncritically take over structures from its own surrounding culture any more than it can uncritically import them from outside. But it can evaluate each structure for its biblical validity and cultural viability. Often it will be found that some indigenous structures (for example, perhaps the family structure) are not at all incompatible with the Church's life and witness, once these structures are given to God.

Third, *church structure must be temporally flexible.* It must be open to modification as changing circumstances warrant.

Here we face not only the spatial but also the temporal dimension. Cultures are dynamic, not static. As they change, changes in church structure will also be necessary. The structure that is effective today may be less so thirty (or even ten) years from now. This is especially true in the modern technological age of discontinuity and rapid change. The fact is that faithfulness to unchanging biblical truth often requires changing structures as time passes.

**Structure in the Early Church**    The book of Acts shows that the early church was not entirely unstructured, although no formal organizational structures existed.[1] The necessary functions of worship, community, leadership, nurture and witness were all provided for. The book of Acts shows that all these needs were recognized and cared for in the early Church:

1. *Worship.* The first Christians did not neglect praise and corporate worship. They worshiped together in the temple courts (Acts 2:46; 5:42), "praising God and enjoying the favor of all the people" (Acts 2:47). Later, of course, when Jewish Christians were barred from Jewish worship and many Gentiles were converted, uniquely Christian worship sprang up. And of course the prayer and fellowship meetings in homes were also worship gatherings.

2. *Community.* The early church was a fellowship or community (*koinonia*). The first Christians "devoted themselves to . . . fellowship" (Acts 2:42). They met as groups in private homes (Acts 2:46; 5:42) and cared for each other's material needs (4:34-35). The home was the center of the common life of the Church during its first two hundred years.

3. *Leadership.* The early church devoted itself "to the *apostles'* teaching" (Acts 2:42). Signs and wonders were done "by the apostles" (Acts 2:43). Leadership initially was in the hands of the original apostles (Acts 4:32-35); later additional leaders also emerged or were chosen. We are reminded that "in the church at Antioch there were prophets and teachers" (Acts 13:1).

4. *Nurture.* The early church devoted itself "to the apostles' *teaching.*" Nurture didn't just happen; Christian truth was consciously taught. The apostles were "standing in the temple

courts teaching the people" (Acts 5:25), among whom were probably many new converts. And even with persecution, "day after day, in the temple courts and from house to house, they never stopped teaching and proclaiming the good news that Jesus is the Christ" (Acts 5:42).

5. *Witness.* The early church clearly had a dramatic evangelistic witness, both through the apostles' proclamation (Acts 4:33; 5:42) and through the example and witness of the larger body of believers (Acts 8:1-4). The power of the proclamation and the power of love demonstrated in community resulted in the Christians at first "enjoying the favor of all the people," and thus "the Lord added to their number daily those who were being saved" (Acts 2:47). To the extent that this witness was verbal, it included preaching in the temple and in private homes, open-air preaching and the daily, person-to-person witness of the multitude of believers. But it was more than verbal; it included service (*diakonia*) as well as proclamation.

All these functional needs were met during the very first days of the Christian Church. As we move on through Acts and throughout the New Testament we find these five functions continually being carried out, although in varying ways. Paul himself constantly preached and taught, established Christian communities, emphasized worship and provided for ongoing leadership.

What kind of structures nourished this varied life of the early church? It is fruitless to try to discover a formal organization underlying the life of the early church. The supposition that the first believers "must have had" a more formal organization than appears in the New Testament is unfounded speculation which says more about our modern mania for getting organized than about what the Church really needs in order to be effective. It is noteworthy that not only is no formalized structure detectible, but also that none is prescribed.

If one goes carefully through the book of Acts with an eye to structure, several things come into view:

First, there is considerable evidence of emerging structures throughout the book. Leaders are chosen or arise; patterns of meeting together emerge; decisions are made. We see a young church developing functional forms as particular needs or problems arise.

Second, there is no formal teaching about structures or no exposition of structures as such; no prescriptions.

Third, some structures and leadership terminology are apparently taken over from Jewish practice, such as the synagogue pattern.

Fourth, new structures are created to meet emerging needs. This is evident especially in chapters 2, 4—6, 12, 13, 15 and 20. It is not always evident, however, whether particular arrangements (such as the choosing of the seven in Acts 6) became fixed patterns or were merely one-time provisions.

Fifth, certain things are plainly absent in Acts—most notably, a formally ordained clergy and a formal constitution or book of discipline. We note that although "a large number of priests became obedient to the faith" (Acts 6:7), there is no evidence that they immediately or automatically became leaders in the Christian community.

Finally, Acts reveals differences in structures in different circumstances. We are not told that the pattern of the Jerusalem church (Acts 2—5) was followed in Antioch, or the pattern of Antioch in Ephesus. Doubtless there were many similarities from place to place, but we may assume that differences and adaptations were common. We see no concern to standardize patterns, nor is any overall structure prescribed for all. Common patterns apparently emerged on the basis of common understandings, but with local adaptations and innovations.

What did the local Christian communities in the first century have in common? What structures helped them carry out necessary functions? From the biblical evidence I have been able to identify very few patterns in the life of the early church which may fairly be called "structures." Of these, the three most general and most basic are charismatic leadership, large-group worship and small-group fellowship.

*Charismatic leadership.* The discussion of spiritual gifts in chapter five has underlined the importance of charismatic leadership for the biblical understanding of the church. The point to emphasize here is that gift-based leadership was, *in practice,* the norm for the early church (not just St. Paul's nice theory!). This may actually be seen as a structure.

In the early church, leadership was essentially a matter of recognizing divinely-appointed leaders through sensitivity to the Spirit's action in giving spiritual gifts. At first there was no formal organizational provision for choosing or replacing leaders; those with leadership gifts exercised them and were recognized as apostles, prophets, evangelists, pastors or teachers. In the local church they were usually called deacons or elders. This, apparently, was the New Testament pattern. Beyond this, no scriptural provisions for leadership structures in the Church can be discerned. So today each local Christian community is free to develop its own leadership patterns, provided these patterns are sensitive to and in harmony with the basic biblical provision of leadership through spiritual gifts.

But isn't "charismatic leadership" fundamentally unstructured? May leadership through spiritual gifts properly be called a structure? Yes, because first of all this is a definite perspective from which to view the matter of leadership; and second, because in the absence of this perspective very definite and fixed patterns rapidly emerge. In any group, it is leadership patterns which become most quickly and firmly institutionalized.

*Large-group and small-group gatherings.* Large-group worship and small-group fellowship are basic, complementary structures. The early church maintained its life and witness by continuing "to meet together in the temple courts" and by breaking bread in believers' homes (Acts 2:46). The two focal points of its life were "in the temple and at home" (Acts 5:42 RSV). This was the pattern both for witness and for sustaining the life that led to witness.

Not all the large-group gatherings were in the temple, of course. We see a winsome freedom from dependence on buildings in the very early church. Sometimes such gatherings were held in larger homes or rooms (Acts 1:13; 12:12), or were open-air meetings (Acts 2:6-14; 3:11).

Where did the early church learn this use of large-group and small-group gatherings? To a large extent it was, of course, simply the natural way to do things. But it is significant that this was the pattern the apostles had followed with Jesus. For two to three years the Twelve had spent most of their time with Jesus either among outdoor crowds, in the temple or in private small-group conferences with him. There was always this harmonious small-group/large-group rhythm, the small group providing the intense community life which gave depth to the large-group gatherings (whether the latter were for worship or for witness).

Here again extensive examples could be cited, both from Paul's ministry and from the first two centuries of church history. We know that Paul utilized the synagogue, open-air gatherings and (at least on one occasion) a lecture hall (Acts 19:9-10). And we know, as well, of Paul's references to house meetings and "the church that meets in your home" (Philem. 2; Col. 4:15; Rom. 16:5; 1 Cor. 16:19).

**Two Patterns**   We, however, are not living in the first century A.D. We look back on the life of the early church through the experience of nearly twenty centuries. Although this is a problem (what do you do with the accumulated weight of two thousand years of ecclesiastical tradition?), it is also an advantage. A careful reading of the intervening centuries should give us a unique perspective from which to examine what happened in those first decades of the Christian era.[2]

Donald Bloesch, in evaluating the impact of the resurgence of Christian communal life in this century, gives us a careful look at varying patterns of Christian discipleship in his book *Wellsprings of Renewal.* Bloesch suggests that while "all Christians are called to holiness or sainthood," still "not all Christians are called to sainthood in the same way." Bloesch believes Scripture presents two patterns of discipleship:

*In biblical and ecclesiastical history two pathways to sanctity can be discerned, and both should be seen as having equal validity in the sight of God. Two patterns of discipleship have arisen, both of which have biblical foundation. On the one hand, there are those who are called to live wholly in the world for the sake of the Gospel, and this entails family life, property, and participation in the affairs of state. . . . On the other hand, some Christians stand under the imperative to fulfill their vocation apart from the world in religious communities or in solitary witness that often entails the renunciation of family, property, and the use of force and violence. Such persons will always be a creative minority, but that they are necessary to the life of the church cannot be denied.*[3]

These comments may be helpful as we look at the question of structure. Bloesch places the current resurgence of Christian communes and other types of intentional communities in the context of the whole monastic tradition. Many of the monastic orders were, at least at their inception, attempts at radical discipleship in terms of both separation from the world and service to the world. The most obvious and, to many, the most appealing example is the Franciscans, followers of St. Francis of Assisi.[4]

The disturbing thing about the suggestion of "two patterns of discipleship"—especially to Protestants—is the implication of a kind of split-level or double-standard ethic which cancels out the tough demands of the gospel for the majority of believers and elevates a minority to a superspiritual elite. This tendency must be rejected. Certainly there cannot be two levels of discipleship. Some are not called to be holier than others, nor can some legitimately be less obedient than others.

But Bloesch is suggesting not two levels but two patterns (structures) of discipleship. If we can admit that all are called to discipleship but not all are called in the same way, we may further our whole understanding of the problem of church structure.

Bloesch calls the various Christian communities which have arisen "in protest against the worldliness of the church" *para-parochial forms*, "since they exist alongside of the parish or institutional church. At the same time it is important that they be in organic relationship with the church lest they become sectarian. . . . A religious community should ideally be an *ecclesiola* (little church) in the ecclesia."[5] Bloesch goes on to suggest seven marks of "a biblically based community or brotherhood in the world today";[6] (1) it should be genuinely evangelical, committed to the gospel and drawing its principal inspiration from the Bible; (2) it should be a small-scale model of the Church, thus visibly demonstrating the reality of the Christian community; (3) it should be an agent of reconciliation between the churches, being in the proper sense catholic as well as evangelical; (4) it should be outreaching, with an evangelistic missionary fervor; (5) it will be in conflict with the principal values and spirit of surrounding culture, thus demonstrating the line between the Church and the world; (6) it should be an eschatological sign of the coming Kingdom of God by its radical witness to the lordship of Christ; and (7) it should give time to study and instruction as well as prayer and proclamation.

In speaking about two patterns of discipleship, Bloesch is really raising the question of church structure. Though not every believer may be called to communal or quasi-communal life, suggests Bloesch, still the Church needs such intentional communities as a basic pattern within its overall structure. Some believers will be especially called to this pattern. Thus there is a place for the smaller, more intimate fellowship or *ecclesiola* within the larger community of the Church. All Christians are called to the same total commitment to Christ, but the members of such a community are more wholly committed to the other members of the group and to the specific mission for which the group exists.

Historian and missiologist Ralph D. Winter has been examining the question of church structure from another perspective. His primary concern is to find those structures which are most effective in spreading the gospel and planting the Church around the world. He presents a thought-provoking analysis of structures for mission that in some ways parallels Bloesch's "two patterns of discipleship."[7]

As the first of "two structures of God's redemptive mission," Winter points to the local church, the basic characteristic of which is that it includes whole families. Such a structure must, therefore, concern itself with the whole range of human concerns. It cannot focus effectively on just one concern, at least not for long.

*In other words, there is something about the nature of the church— whether a local structure, a nationwide denomination, an international communion or an entire church tradition (e.g., family of churches)—that vitally depends upon human wholeness. The glory of the church, even a local church, is that it patiently endeavors to foster balanced, redemptive community across the whole span of ages, the differences in sex, even differences in station in life.*[8]

In contrast, Winter points to a second "redemptive structure" which is more restricted. Taking an Inter-Varsity Christian Fellowship chapter as an example, Winter says such a group "exists expressly (and urgently) to fulfill the need for homogeneous worship and fellowship, but thereby precisely falls short of the other continuing need for heterogeneous

worship and fellowship." The function of such a more restricted group may be contrasted with the broader role of the
church: "The church, then, characteristically preserves the
wholesome *unity* of the human community while the men's
Bible class, the women's association, the church school class
and the youth group manifest the wholesome *diversity* of the
human community."[9]

Winter believes these two structures—one more inclusive
and general, the other more restricted and potentially mission-oriented—can be traced down through church history,
even going back to New Testament days.[10] The early church
community borrowed its basic structure from the synagogue:
"Let us recognize the structure so fondly called 'The New
Testament Church' as basically a Christian synagogue."[11] The
new churches planted by Paul, in particular, were "essentially
built along Jewish synagogue lines, embracing the community
of the faithful in any given place."[12] The really unique thing
about these new communities was their ability through the
reconciling work of Christ to break down "the dividing wall of
hostility" between Jew and Gentile and bring both together in
one open fellowship (Eph. 2:11-22). The common pattern of
the church in the New Testament was a synagogue type of
community which (as I have contended above) centered
around large-group corporate worship and small-group fellowship and worship cells meeting primarily in homes.

But Winter sees a second, more restricted structure at work
in the New Testament, especially in Paul's missionary work:
*While we know very little about the structure of the evangelistic out-
reach within which pre-Pauline Jewish proselytizers worked, we do
know . . . that they operated all over the Roman Empire. It would be
surprising if Paul didn't follow somewhat the same procedures. And
we know a great deal more about the way Paul operated. He was, true
enough, sent out by the church in Antioch. But once away from
Antioch he seemed very much on his own. The little team he formed
was economically self-sufficient when occasion demanded. It was also*

*dependent, from time to time, not alone upon the Antioch church, but upon other churches that had risen as a result of evangelistic labors. Paul's team may certainly be considered a structure.*[13]

In other words, Paul borrowed from Judaism both the synagogue and the structure of a missionary band. These provided the pattern in his church planting and missionary ministry. Thus, according to Winter, "Paul's *missionary band* can be considered a prototype of all subsequent missionary endeavors organized out of committed, experienced workers who affiliated themselves as a second decision beyond membership in the first structure."[14]

This additional second-choice, task-oriented structure maintained a link with the Antioch church, but it was semiautonomous. Since it was composed of a smaller group of adults all committed to the same mission, it had the freedom and flexibility to carry out its mission (evangelism and church planting) much more effectively than the larger community acting as a whole could do.

What happened as the early church became dominant throughout the Roman Empire? Winter sees the same pattern of two complementary structures continuing, but in different ways. The parish church within a diocese developed throughout the empire and "still preserved the basic constituency of the synagogue, namely, the combination of old and young, male and female—that is, a biologically perpetuating organism." Meanwhile "the monastic tradition in various early forms, developed as a second structure."[15] Thus,

*there are already by the fourth century two very different kinds of structure—the diocese and the monastery—both of them significant in the transmission and expansion of Christianity. They are each patterns borrowed from the cultural context of their time, just as were the earlier Christian synagogue and missionary band.*[16]

Many Protestants almost instinctively react against monasticism, but their reaction is usually against the decadent form of monasticism which existed at the time of the Reformation.

Early monasticism, despite an unfortuante dualism in theology, was often highly creative and socially reformatory. In any case, the conversion of much of Europe was due to a great extent to the monastic orders, and many medieval renewal movements began within these orders or led to the founding of new ones. So without justifying all the theology involved, one can at least point out the utility of the structure and cite it as one example of a more restricted, task-oriented group.

Winter draws one final historical parallel: the rise of the independent missionary societies during the past one hundred years, to which the founding of hundreds of new Christian churches around the world has been largely due. Again, the structure is outwardly different from either the New Testament missionary band or the medieval monastic or preaching order, but one can note the functional equivalence and ponder the significance of the parallel.

The principal point of contact between Bloesch's "two patterns of discipleship" and Winter's "two structures of mission" is the recognition of the practical utility of a more restricted, second-decision, committed fellowship for carrying out the Christian mission in the world. Both argue (correctly, I believe) that these two structures are justified biblically and find numerous precedents throughout the history of the Church.

We are dealing here with structures for mission. This means structuring the community of God's people in such a way that it most effectively serves as the agent of the Kingdom, carrying out those tasks "which God prepared in advance." The quite different analyses of Bloesch and Winter, plus my own experience and reflection, convince me of the need within the larger church community for smaller, more restricted mission-oriented groups. This is true at the local level, certainly, and also at denominational and broader levels. Within the local church, for instance, Christians concerned about specific needs or interested in particular ministries could profitably band together as mission groups, functioning as small-group fellowships around that specific ministry or mission. Gordon Cosby has recently spelled out how such groups can function in his book, *Handbook for Mission Groups,* which draws upon his extensive experience with mission groups in the innovative Church of the Savior in Washington, D.C.[17]

At denominational, regional and other levels similar special-ministry structures are useful. These may take the form of semiautonomous missionary/church-planting societies, as suggested by Winter, or they may be in the form of intentional communities committed to some kind of Christian social ministry, as cited by Bloesch. Such groups may be totally independent from existing denominations or may be denominationally affiliated. The important points are that these structures (1) consist of people committed to each other and to a particular mission and (2) see themselves not as the Church but as an "order" or missionary structure within the Church, with which they remain in fellowship and communication.

On the local level, one can imagine the following scenario. Several different small-group fellowships are functioning within the larger community of the church. These are task-oriented or mission groups, each existing for a specific but different purpose. While Bible study, prayer and sharing are common to all groups, each group also has a very specific mission for which it exists and to which it is dedicated.

Thus on Wednesday evening, for instance, at the church building, the music fellowship has just completed its Bible study and prayer time and is into a music planning session. Some of the group members will be meeting later in the week for rehearsal. Across town another dozen people are meeting in a member's house. This is the missions fellowship. The group has shared in prayer concerning recent requests from the mission field and now is busy with the planning and implementation of the church's missionary program. Simultaneously in another home the social reform fellowship is studying a piece of legislation which has come up in Congress, in order to know what the church's response should be. Meanwhile, two of the evangelistic visitation teams are out in the community and another is involved in a follow-up Bible study. Not all the task groups are meeting tonight, however; the multimedia, Christian nurture and other fellowships meet at other times.[18]

The advantages of this arrangement are many. In particular, such mission groups offer the following positive features:

First, the mission group arrangement recognizes and allows for diversity of personalities and spiritual gifts. Not all Christians are called to the same specific task, nor do they all have the same spiritual gifts. "Having gifts that differ according to the grace given to us, let us use them" (Rom. 12:6, RSV). It is a tragedy to try to force every believer into the same ministry, as though all had the same place in the body; it is an even greater tragedy when gifts go unused. Mission groups provide a structure compatible with spiritual gifts.

Second, the mission group arrangement recognizes that certain tasks are so urgent and of such high priority as to demand the total commitment of a few dedicated people. Thus this structure provides for a proper recognition of priorities and a practical way of responding significantly to priority needs. It is more effective and less frustrating to get a small group involved with a specific mission than to attempt to get a large number of people stirred up and committed to that task.

Third, this arrangement also recognizes that mission is best carried out in the context of community. The lone entrepreneur and the rugged individualist do not exemplify the proper model for Christian service. The biblical Christian is called both to community and to mission. This is biblical and it is psychologically realistic. While there is a legitimate place for the strong leader, that leadership should work through a small-group community which allows for team leadership and shared tasks. Effective Christian service is always Jesus Christ working through his own body, doing the works he did while on earth.

Fourth, the mission group arrangement meets the need for both homogeneous and heterogeneous fellowship and worship.[19] The Church must be a reconciling fellowship which cuts across barriers of sex, social status, age, racial and ethnic backgrounds, and economic standing. Nevertheless, some tasks are best carried out by groups which are in one respect or another more homogeneous. Such an arrangement holds together unity and diversity, homogeneity and heterogeneity, in a way that allows the body of Christ to be what God intended it to be.

Finally, for the above reasons, mission groups are often more effective in accomplishing certain tasks and reaching specific goals than lone individuals, appointed committees and boards, or the whole church community in general. The mission group has a higher level of commitment with regard to the specific mission involved. It concentrates and focuses the light of the gospel so that it cuts through to the goal. Its fewer members, high level of commitment and freedom from other concerns (since it is not encumbered with the whole weight of the church program) give it an enviable flexibility which heightens effectiveness.

All mission groups, however, must be tied in to the body. Each group, really a subcommunity, functions as part of the larger community of the church. Much harm can be done to the body by a small group with an independent spirit which goes off on a tangent and creates division. There must therefore be coordination among such structures, both on the local level and more broadly. In a local church community, at least one person from each group, with some gifts for leadership, should participate in a coordinating group which acts as a clearing-house for information and a center for ideas and planning. Thus the groups are mutually supportive, each contributing to the other, demonstrating in still another respect the mutuality of the body of Christ.

Similarly, each group is not to carry out its specific mission in total isolation or independence from other groups. All groups are part of the body. Cooperation is needed between the groups to achieve maximum effectiveness. This is true within a local church community and the same thing applies to several local churches within a city or suburb. James F. Engel and H. Wilbert Norton in their book *What's Gone Wrong with the Harvest?* demonstrate the need for such cooperation and show how to go about it.[20] This cooperation is equally necessary at regional, national and world levels where cooperative planning and coordination is notoriously lacking among missionary societies, evangelistic organizations and similar groups. As David McKenna suggests, too often in the Church "a wide span . . . exists between brothers who share a common faith and partners who are willing to share common resources."[21]

Structuring the Church, both locally and more generally, on the basis of discerned tasks and discovered spiritual gifts is one way to a more charismatic/organic church structure, which is both more true to the New Testament picture of the Church and more functional in a technological society. Properly conceived and followed through, it is a way to circumvent institutionalism and avoid the deadening effects of impersonal programs and promotions.

But a cautionary word should be added at this point. It is all too easy for the average nominal, well-institutionalized Christian to say, "Yes, that's fine: two structures of discipleship. You take the hard road and I'll take the easy road. Costly discipleship may be your thing, but it's not mine."

Clearly, this will not do. A person is either a disciple of Jesus Christ or no Christian at all. A believer either experiences costly, close *koinonia* with brothers and sisters in Christ or he or she has only the foggiest of notions as to what the Church is all about.

And yet, not all Jesus' disciples were among the Twelve who left all and followed him. To each disciple is given a different gift and a different way of ministry. Some are even given the gift of celibacy (1 Cor. 7:1-7). But all, without exception and to the same degree, are called to discipleship.

We may therefore introduce two qualifications of what has been said in the preceding pages. First, all Christians should be involved in some form of small-group sharing built around the Word. I am not talking here about shallow fellowship groups, but about cells of true *koinonia* where believers take costly responsibility for each other as they live their lives in the world.

Second, we must not confuse any historical expressions of discipleship patterns with the biblical norm. We can learn, for example, from monasticism, from contemporary missionary structures or from New Testament examples. But none of these is being held up here as the perfect model to be imitated today. Above all, we must avoid the split-level view of discipleship which has often compromised the Church's witness in the past. The Church's task today is to find those patterns of obedience which recognize differences in calling on the one hand and the universal summons to discipleship and obedience on the other.

**The Church and Institutional Structures**   The discussion of the charismatic versus the institutional dimension of the Church in chapter four emphasized that the Church will inevitably assume some institutional forms, even though the Church is not the institution. It will be helpful to say more about the differences between the Church as the community of God's people, as presented in Scripture, and all supportive institutional or para-church structures which exist ostensibly to serve the Church.

When we look at the contemporary Church, we see not only the community of God's people; we find also a proliferation of local church organizations, denominations, institutions, agencies, associations and so forth. Such structures obviously have no explicit biblical basis. How should we view them?

The two most common tendencies have been either to say these structures are actually a part of the essence of the Church, and thus sacralize them, or to take an anti-institutional stance and say all such structures are invalid and must be abandoned. The first option is essentially that of traditional Roman Catholic ecclesiology, although many Protestants have unwittingly adopted the same view. The second option is popular among those who have seen the blemishes of institutional Christianity and who, like Bill at the beginning of this chapter, think institutionless Christianity is somehow possible.

A more helpful option, however, is to view all institutional structures as para-church structures which exist alongside of and parallel to the community of God's people but are not themselves the Church. Such structures have three things in common: they are structured institutionally rather than organically or charismatically; they exist alongside or parallel to the church community; and they exist ostensibly to serve the Church.

Para-church structures are useful to the extent that they aid the Church in its mission, but are manmade and culturally determined. Whereas the Church itself is part of the new wine of the gospel, all para-church structures are wineskins—useful, at times indispensable, but also subject to wear and decay.

In dealing with the whole question of church structure, then, it is helpful to make a clear distinction between the Church as the community of God's people and all para-church structures, whether local church organizational forms, denominational structures, mission agencies, evangelistic organizations, educational institutions or other ecclesiastical structures (Figure 5). Thus the Church is a spiritual reality which is always cross-culturally valid. But para-church

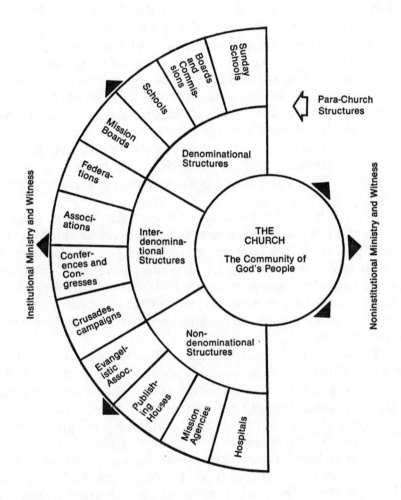

**Figure 5.** The Church and Para-Church Structures

structures are not the essence of the Church. Believers within these structures, in their common life as a people and a community, are the Church. When such para-church structures are confused with the Church, or seen as part of its essence, all kinds of unfortunate misunderstandings result, and we bind the Church to its particular cultural and structural expression.

Several benefits come from this distinction between the Church and para-church structures. (1) That which is always cross-culturally relevant (the Church) is distinguished from that which is culturally bound and determined (para-church structures). Thus, one is free to see the Church as culturally relevant and involved and yet not as culturally bound. (2) One is free also to modify para-church structures as culture changes, for these are not themselves the Church and therefore are, for the most part, culturally rather than biblically determined. (3) Finally, this distinction makes it possible to see a wide range of legitimacy in denominational confessions and structures. If such structures are not themselves the Church and are culturally determined, then whole volumes of controversy and polemics lose their urgency and become merely secondary. Widely varying confessions are freed (at least potentially) to concentrate on that which unites them, namely, being the people of God and carrying out their kingdom tasks, while relegating structural differences to the plane of cultural and historical relativity. Thus the crucial consideration for structure becomes not biblical legitimacy but functional relevancy.

Table 3 suggests further implications of this distinction between the biblical Church and para-church structures. For the sake of analysis, the differences between the two are set in sharper relief here than normally occurs in the concrete instance.

I would emphasize that this distinction is not merely a restatement of the visible/invisible understanding of the

Church. The Church is both visible and invisible and so are para-church structures; even a secular organization has its invisible dimensions, as Jacques Ellul has pointed out.[22] I am

| The Church | Para-Church Structures |
|---|---|
| 1. God's creation | 1. Man's creation |
| 2. Spiritual fact | 2. Sociological fact |
| 3. Cross-culturally valid | 3. Culturally bound |
| 4. Biblically understood and evaluated | 4. Sociologically understood and evaluated |
| 5. Validity determined by spiritual qualities and fidelity to Scriptures | 5. Validity determined by function in relation to mission of the Church |
| 6. God's agent of evangelism and reconciliation | 6. Man's agents for evangelism and service |
| 7. Essential | 7. Expendable |
| 8. Eternal | 8. Temporal and temporary |
| 9. Divine revelation | 9. Human tradition |
| 10. Purpose to glorify God | 10. Purpose to serve the Church |

**Table 3.** Differences between the Church and Para-Church Structures

distinguishing, rather, between the Church as biblically understood and auxiliary ecclesiastical structures which did not exist normatively in New Testament days but which have appeared in many forms down through church history. These are para-church, for to say any particular structures are theologically necessary to the Church's being would be to say the first-century church was not truly and completely the Church.

The term *para-church structures* has customarily been used to designate nondenominational and interdenominational organizations such as Inter-Varsity Christian Fellowship, Campus Crusade for Christ, World Vision or a council of churches. But the attempt to make a biblical (rather than merely pragmatic) analysis of this question encounters a basic difficulty in this traditional understanding. There is no biblical basis for a fundamental distinction between denominational structures and para-denominational organizations; nor is there any basis for considering obviously man-made denominational organizations, which are a relatively recent development in church history, as essential to the Church. In other words, the more basic distinction seems to be between the Church as the body of Christ, the community of God's people, and all institutional structures, including denominations. Ralph Winter has suggested calling such structures *infra-church structures* to emphasize their subordinate but supporting relationship to the Church, and to avoid making a complete break between the Christian community and its structures.

My conviction is that the Protestant view of Scripture and revelation does not allow us to include denominational or other organizational structures not found in the Bible as actually part of the Church itself. There is a fundamental difference here between Protestant and traditional Roman Catholic views of the Church, although the implications of the Reformation in this area of ecclesiology have never been carried through to their logical conclusion. Protestants who distinguish between biblical revelation and church tradition should have no difficulty making a distinction between the biblical Church and institutional church structures. The categories are parallel. The biblical Church is grounded in biblical revelation; para-church or infra-church structures are based in postbiblical church tradition.

Isn't this Church/para-church distinction merely another way of distinguishing between people and organization? In one sense, yes. The Church is *the people* of God. But this people, to be the Church, must live in community through appropriate structures and through the exercise of spiritual gifts—regardless of the institutional organizations within which they secondarily may be involved. Once we distinguish between ecclesiastical institutional structures and the Church as the people of God (drawing the line of demarcation there rather than between the denomination or local church and nondenominational ministries), then we can see more clearly how effective ministry can and should be carried out.

Biblically speaking it is irrelevant, for instance, whether evangelism is carried out by a denomination or by some non-denominational structure. In both cases the sponsoring structure is in reality a para-church structure, not the Church itself. It is not fundamentally important whether foreign missions (to take another example) are carried out by denominational mission boards or by independent missionary agencies. Both forms of ministry may be equally valid or invalid, depending on whether they do in fact actually extend and build the community of God's people.

Evangelism, regardless of the agency which sponsors it, is legitimate only as it plants and edifies the Church or extends its witness. All social ministry, regardless of its sponsoring structure, is biblically valid only as it is in some way an authentic expression of the community of God's people. Evangelistic and missionary efforts which form new Christian communities or add to those already formed are legitimate if they really build the Church as biblically understood. If they do not, they are a waste of effort, regardless of how they are structured or of the biblical legitimacy they claim. Of course it is fundamentally important that all ministry, whether evangelistic or prophetic, take care to contribute to the visible and spiritual unity, rather than disunity, of the body of Christ.

The important thing for every form of ministry is that the biblical Church be built and grow to maturity in Christ, that is, that local Christian communities or fellowships be multiplied, that such communities truly demonstrate the quality of life seen in Jesus Christ, and that the Church live in the world as the redeemed people of God. From a biblical point of view,

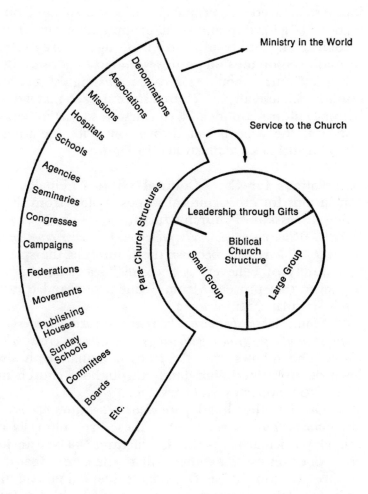

**Figure 6.** A Model for Church Structure

questions of denominational or nondenominational affilia-
tion or structure are strictly secondary.

In summary, the Church as the community of God's people
is best structured on spiritual gifts of leadership and on some
form of large-group and small-group gatherings. It should
recognize the utility of, and encourage, more restricted,
second-decision mission groups within its larger self. Beyond
this, the Church should take care to distinguish between its
essential self and all para-church structures so that it does not
become culture-bound, and, conversely, so that in periods of
upheaval the wine is not thrown out with the wineskins.
These principles are illustrated in Figure 6.

**Implications for Cross-Cultural Witness**  Finally, several
conclusions for cross-cultural witness follow from the foregoing discussion of church structure.

1. *The Church as biblically presented is always cross-culturally
relevant.* This is true because the Church as the space-time
community of believers is a cosmic/historical, charismatic
organism that proceeds from divine action and transcends
any particular cultural form.

2. Similarly, *the basic structures of charismatic leadership and
small-group/large-group gatherings are always cross-culturally
viable.* This follows from the foregoing analysis; it also has
been demonstrated abundantly throughout church history
and in the modern missionary age.

3. On the other hand, *para-church structures are not necessarily cross-culturally valid.* Since these are culturally determined, particular para-church structures will be transferable
from one culture to another only to the extent that the two
cultures are compatible. Often basic adaptations will have to
be made. Missionaries must be concerned with the transfer
and implantation of the Church as biblically described, not
with the reproduction of secondary institutions or forms
which are really nothing other than para-church structures.

4. *The exercise of spiritual gifts will result in cross-cultural evangelism and witness.* Since the first Gentile outreach recorded in the book of Acts and through the ages, God has been calling and sending forth his charismatically equipped missionaries. The Antiochene pattern (Acts 13:1-3) has been repeated countless times and will continue to be repeated until Christ returns (Mt. 24:14). It is God who calls and who gives gifts, and the gift and the call go together.

5. *The Church is itself a missionary community, and any group of missionaries may be a legitimate embodiment of the Church.* This means there can be no question of the Church versus missionary structures. Wherever missionaries are, there is the Church and there missionaries are responsible for demonstrating the reality of Christian community. The real point of tension therefore is between the Church as the community of God's people and institutional expressions of the Church. Missionaries can never go to another culture and leave the Church behind! But they can, and often should, leave behind or modify the para-church forms peculiar to their own culture.

6. On the other hand, *para-church missionary/evangelistic structures should be created wherever needed to get the job done.* While the Church is God's agent of evangelism, dynamic para-church structures can be man's agents of evangelism, useful in God's hands for the more rapid and effective propagation of the gospel. Denominational groups should freely collaborate with other para-church organizations which are doing work they themselves cannot do, or which will help them carry on their own evangelistic work. Such organizations, however, should always be directed ultimately toward the formation of the Church (though in widely different ways), while not allowing themselves to be confused with the Church or to become ends in themselves.

7. Since they are manmade and culturally determined, *all para-church structures should be subjected to continuous rigorous*

*sociological and theological analysis* to determine their effectiveness as instruments of the Church. We should not hesitate to make the most exacting sociological studies of mission agencies, evangelistic movements, social reform groups and denominational structures. History teaches us that many such structures will eventually succumb to institutionalism and become hindrances to the gospel rather than helps. The fact that God has raised up a movement is no warranty against eventual infidelity or idolatry. Having clearly distinguished such structures from the essence of the Church, we can freely ask to what extent these forms are actually functioning without fearing we are somehow desecrating holy things.[23]

In the final analysis, church structure is a question of the community of God's people using their God-given intelligence and creativity to manufacture useful tools to help extend the Church's witness, while always remembering that these manmade tools stand under God's judgment and must never be worshiped.

# THE UNITY
## OF THE CHURCH

The local church is always part of the one, holy, apostolic, universal Church of Jesus Christ. It must be seen in this larger perspective to be rightly understood. In one sense the Church is fully present in each local community of believers, for Jesus Christ is there. But each local church also participates in the one people of God scattered throughout the world.

So we turn now to the question of the unity of the Church. In chapter two we commented on some things which the Lausanne Covenant (produced by the 1974 International Congress on World Evangelization) said about the nature of the Church. We begin now by noting what the Covenant said about the unity of the Church, under the title "Cooperation in Evangelism."

*We affirm that the church's visible unity in truth is God's purpose. Evangelism also summons us to unity, because our oneness strengthens our witness, just as our disunity undermines our gospel of reconciliation. We recognize, however, that organizational unity may take many forms and does not necessarily forward evangelism. Yet we who share the same biblical faith should be clearly united in fellowship, work and witness. We confess that our testimony has sometimes been marred by sinful individualism and needless duplication. We pledge ourselves to seek a deeper unity in truth, worship, holiness and mission.*[1]

Participants at the 1974 International Congress on World Evangelization in Lausanne rejoiced in the unity they felt as they shared together for ten days. Diverse cultures, languages and ecclesiastical traditions were temporarily blended as Christian believers shared in worship, fellowship, study and dialog, united by the same vital faith in Jesus Christ.

That very real and valid experiential joy of being together, however, should not blind us today to three fundamental facts which bear on the whole question of cooperation in evangelism and the worldwide witness of the Church. (1) The Lausanne experience was made possible because flesh-and-blood believers came together at a particular time and place. (2) The unity, while real, was temporary; it continues to exist more as memory than as present fact. (3) This unity, while based in the transcendent gospel, was made possible by the Congress, which was a specific manmade, space-time structure with various committees and supporting groups. Unity was experienced because a specific enabling structure was created.

It is well to bear these observations in mind as we consider the problem of the unity of the Church.

**Unity: An Expression of the Gospel** Oneness is a fundamental and essential characteristic of the gospel. Biblical faith rests on this basic affirmation: "The LORD our God is one LORD; and you shall love the LORD your God with all your heart, and with all your soul, and with all your might" (Dt. 6:4-5; see Mk. 12:29-30). The Bible insists that there is but one God, that God is one and all that exists comes from his hands. Scripture radically rejects any ontological dualism (whether between good and evil or between spirit and matter) by beginning with God and making the entire universe dependent on God's creative Word. God and the universe are distinguishable, and only God is eternal.

In contrast, all nonbiblical philosophy and religion is fundamentally dualistic.[2] In rejecting revealed truth humanity tends to push the present problem of evil clear back to eternity and to make all reality eternally dichotomous. Such dualism is behind all nonbiblical thinking and has often infected Christian theology.

The fact that God is one provides the foundation for the New Testament emphasis on the unity of the gospel and of the Church. "There is one body and one Spirit—just as you were called to one hope when you were called—one Lord, one faith, one baptism; one God and Father of all, who is over all and through all and in all" (Eph. 4:4-6). There is thus a certain "giveness" to the Church's unity. The gospel is one and there is but one gospel for it is the revealed truth of the one God. And yet the very fact that the Church is, by nature, one, if not understood biblically, can easily lead to a Platonic dualism between an ideal Church (which is truly and safely one) and the real church on earth. The latter is in fact fragmented but we think we need not be concerned about this because, after all, the ideal, "spiritual" Church is inalterably one, which is what really matters—or so we think.

Because there is one God there is but one gospel. And because there is but one gospel there is but one Church. Jesus Christ is one and the Church is his one body. Faced with factions in the Corinthian church Paul asked, "Is Christ divided?" (1 Cor. 1:13). He is not, either in head or body. And yet the space-time reality of the Church too often fails to show this unity—just as happened in first-century Corinth. Many groups "profess to be followers of the Lord but they differ in mind and go their different ways, as if Christ Himself were divided."[3]

Evangelicals have no trouble affirming the unity of God and even of the gospel, but often we get into difficulty with respect to the Church. What does "one Lord, one faith, one baptism" mean in practical terms when we are confronted with the reality of the Church in history?

Insofar as that segment of the Church which calls itself

evangelical has difficulty with the unity of the Church, it betrays a theological problem which evangelicals have yet to deal with adequately: the doctrine of the Church.[4] The fact is that Protestantism has never developed a fully biblical doctrine of the Church. Protestantism (and thus contemporary evangelicalism) operates with an often confused and somewhat Platonic view of the Church which undercuts the possibility of arriving at a biblically sound solution to many problems related to the Church's nature and mission. This is true whether the problem be unity, evangelism, social witness or whatever. The only solution therefore is to return to Scripture and self-consciously dig out a biblical ecclesiology that does not conflict with biblical soteriology; which sees ecclesiology and soteriology as one, and the Church as part of the gospel.

Roman Catholic ecclesiology is based on the twin pillars of Scripture and tradition. But tradition has generally meant the predominance of the institutional over the charismatic in the experience and doctrine of the Church.[5] Too often conservative Protestants have tacitly accepted this way of conceiving the body of Christ. The result is a hang-up over the question of organizational versus spiritual unity, which sees these as almost mutually exclusive categories. Because of the excesses of Roman Catholicism and of the ecumenical movement, many evangelicals tend to reject outright any talk of organizational unity and are satisfied with a vague, indefinable "spiritual" unity which consequently has very little practical and historical significance. Henri Blocher is right in saying that "invisible unity must be expressed in a visible way." His question, "Haven't we fallen into an easy self-satisfaction when we have acclaimed our spiritual unity?" can be answered in the affirmative.[6]

The recovery of a biblical understanding of the Church will mean the ability to see that spiritual unity and organizational (or better, structural) unity are different, but not necessarily antithetical. The options are not merely either to accept the

Church as essentially institutional (the traditional Roman Catholic view) or else to reject the validity of, and thus the need for, all organizational unity. Organizational and institutional structures have their functional validity, provided they are seen as para-church structures and are not sacralized.

That there is but one God and one gospel means there can also be but one Church of Jesus Christ. But the affirmation *one Church* must be understood biblically. There is but one people of God on earth, and it is as the people of God that the Church is one.[7] This is much more than an invisible, spiritual unity. This oneness must not be shunted off into "eternity" for it exists in space and time, though imperfectly, and for both theological and practical reasons it must be given some structural expression. The unity of the Church is therefore required as an expression of the gospel itself. The Church must in fact be "one in the Spirit."

Twice the statement on "Cooperation in Evangelism" in the Lausanne Covenant (quoted above) uses the phrase, "unity in truth." Unity in truth is unity in Jesus Christ, who is the truth. He is, in fact, the incarnate truth. So the Church's unity in truth means incarnating the truth of Jesus Christ in today's world and cultures.

John 17 is especially helpful here. Several things stand out in Christ's prayer for the unity of the Church.

First, *the primary purpose of the unity of the Church is that God may be glorified.* Jesus prays, "Glorify your Son, that your Son may glorify you" (Jn. 17:1). Christ's overarching concern, here as always, is that God the Father may be glorified. Eight times Jesus refers to this in his prayer. Christ prays for the unity and the witness of his disciples in order that God may receive glory. Jesus says of his followers in verse 10, "Glory has come to me through them." This is, above all else, the purpose and aim of the Church. God's people are called to live "for the praise of his glory" (Eph. 1:12); "to him be glory in the church and in Christ Jesus" (Eph. 3:21). As Peter Beyerhaus reminds us, "Today it is extremely important to emphasize the priority of this doxological aim before all other aims of mission."[8]

*The secondary purpose for the unity of the Church is the authentic communication of the good news.* This is stated most clearly in verses 21 and 23. Jesus prays that all his followers "may be one, Father, just as you are in me and I am in you. May they also be in us so that the world may believe that you have sent me. . . . I in them and you in me. May they be brought to complete unity to let the world know that you sent me and have loved them even as you have loved me." The Church must demonstrate "unity in truth" so that the good news may be credible.

Third, *unity in truth is unity with Christ and thus with the Trinity.* Jesus' prayer is "that they may be one as we are one" (v. 11). This unity is "I in them and you in me" (v. 23). Further, the same kind of unity that exists between the persons of the Trinity is to be found within the Church and between Christ and the Church. The Church is to be one "just as you are in me and I am in you" (v. 21). The key word in this whole prayer is *as.* We should especially note verse 18, "As you sent me into the world, I have sent them into the world" (compare Jn. 17:18). The Church is to demonstrate within itself and in relation to Jesus Christ the same quality of relationship that exists between Jesus Christ and God the Father. This is unity in truth—true unity.

Finally, *this unity in truth means both unity in belief and unity of life; both orthodoxy and orthopraxis.* Unity in truth means unity in belief. Christians share the same hope, the same faith (Eph. 4:4-5). Christ prays for his disciples because they have received and kept his words (Jn. 17:6-8). The key statement is verse 17: "Sanctify them by the truth; your word is truth." Unity in truth is unity in the Word of God and the words of Christ. Four times here Jesus speaks of the word he has received from the Father and transmitted to his disciples. What

Christ shared with his followers had true content that could be communicated; it was not merely existential, supra-rational experience. Significantly, Christ prays "for those who will believe in me through their message" (v. 20), not just through their life. Evangelism involves communication of a message. And unity in truth must be grounded in basic agreement as to the content of that message.

But unity in truth also means unity of life. It means orthopraxis, or what Francis Schaeffer has called "orthodoxy of community." The Incarnation calls for a living out in daily experience the implications of revealed truth. This also is involved in the prayer, "Sanctify them by the truth" (v. 17). Christ's followers are sent into the world as Jesus himself was: as incarnate truth (v. 18). His disciples are to be known by the love (v. 26) and joy (v. 13) they demonstrate. The Church being one in Christ as Christ is one with the Father certainly means more than mere doctrinal agreement. The cross must be taken as the basis not only of soteriology but of ethics as well.[9] "There is no biblical dichotomy between the Word spoken and the Word made visible in the lives of God's people. Men will look as they listen and what they see must be at one with what they hear."[10] Both unity and evangelism involve much more than merely transmitting what Samuel Escobar has called "verbal summaries" of the gospel.

The unity of the Church, especially on a broad scale, will certainly not involve agreement at every point of doctrine, practice or methodology. But it must be based on unity in truth in both its verbal and incarnational dimensions.

**An Evangelical Ecumenism**   As already noted, Jesus himself underlined the pragmatic importance of unity for witness when he prayed "that all of them may be one, . . . so that the world may believe that you have sent me" (Jn. 17:21).

Strangely, evangelistic and missionary concern among evangelicals has often tended more toward fragmentation than toward unity. Those most deeply concerned about evangelism are often most adamantly opposed to, or else indifferent toward, the practical questions of unity. For the sake of effective evangelism we ought to consider more seriously Jesus' prayer for unity.

If both evangelism and the glory of God summon us to unity, this question becomes a greater concern of earnest Christians than it has been until now. Evangelicals would do well to consider what Donald G. Bloesch has written in his chapter on Christian unity in *The Reform of the Church*. Says Bloesch,

*The goal of authentic ecumenism is not a super-church with power and prestige but rather a worldwide fellowship of believers united under the Word and dedicated to the conversion and salvation of mankind. What we should aim for is . . . an evangelical ecumenism which places Christian mission above institutional survival.*[11]

The goal of such an "evangelical ecumenism," says Bloesch, "would not simply be the unity of the church but also and above all the conversion of the world."[12] The missionary motive, rather than being an excuse for continuing fragmentation, must be the reason for evangelical convergence.[13] At present most ecumenists seem concerned with unity for its own sake and unconcerned about evangelism (in the biblical sense), while too many evangelicals appear concerned with evangelism in itself but are little preoccupied with evangelistically necessary unity and cooperation. Bloesch's call for an evangelical ecumenism is timely.

It would appear that most evangelicals are not really convinced that cooperation and unity are essential for effective evangelism. If they are so convinced, we may legitimately ask, Where is the evidence? There are few visible signs of unity today, other than evangelistic crusades or similar efforts which are essentially exceptional and short-term and are usually only marginally connected to the Church. The tendency, of course, is to discount such a lack by affirming the

Church's "invisible, spiritual unity."

I suggest that the problem here, again, is the problem of our understanding of the Church. Lack of a sufficiently biblical view of the Church produces two results: first, the tendency to limit the whole question of unity to the invisible/spiritual dimension, and second, the tendency of efforts at cooperation to be only marginally related to the actual edification of the Church.

Which is essential to effective gospel proclamation—cooperative evangelistic efforts or the visible unity of the Church itself? Which is more crucial—unity in evangelism or the unity of the people of God? Will the world be convinced more readily by united evangelistic efforts or by the corporate unity of the Church as God's people?

This is not an either/or question, of course. Certainly cooperative evangelism is to be encouraged. But such evangelism must be integrally related to the life and edification of local communities of believers. The principal problem with cooperative efforts up to now is that such efforts have been largely unrelated to the daily ongoing community life of the Church. They have been a special, extraordinary, intensive, added-on program that could not be integrated into the daily experience of specific local Christian congregations. It is now generally recognized that this was a major weakness of the early Evangelism in Depth crusades.[14] Whether it also has been a weakness of the somewhat differently structured "Here's Life America" endeavor remains to be determined.

The evangelistic-missionary mandate summons the Church today toward more effective cooperative efforts in evangelism and also toward some form of visible unity of the Church itself. And in both cases, unity becomes not only a problem of concept but also a problem of structure.

In his high priestly prayer Jesus prays for the oneness of all believers, not merely for "cooperation in evangelism." Jesus was concerned about the unity of the Church, and Christians

today must share this concern. But any valid evangelical
ecumenism must be based not on evangelistic pragmatism
but, even more basically, on a clear biblical understanding of
the Church.

Neither evangelism nor ecumenism is an entity in itself.
Both are aspects of the Church's life in the world. And they
both are defined by the biblical mandate of the Church and
the gospel. When both evangelism and ecumenism are defined on the basis of the biblical understanding of the Church
(that is, of ecclesiology and not just soteriology narrowly conceived), then the essential interrelatedness of these two concerns will become apparent.

I suggest, therefore, that both the evangelistic mandate and
the ecumenical motive summon the contemporary Church to
a new quest for the biblical understanding of the people of
God. The ecclesiological question needs to be investigated
further to provide an adequate basis for the future development of evangelistic and ecumenical concerns.

**A Problem of Structure**   I have emphasized that the International Congress on World Evangelization was a specific,
manmade structure. Further, it was made possible in large
measure by the existence and resources of another major
evangelical structure: the Billy Graham Evangelistic Association.

Cooperation and unity do not "just happen" apart from
enabling structures. God works today, as he has throughout
history, not only through human beings but also through human structures. Cooperation and the unity of the Church are,
therefore, also problems of structure. The question is, What
kinds of structures can and should be created to further the
oneness of the true Church and the effective proclamation
of the gospel?

*Structures for the cooperation and unity of the various communi-
ties of the one people of God should be created at various levels.* Cul-

tural diversity dictates considerable variety in the worship and community lifestyle of the Church, but at each level this diversity should be transcended by some visible structures for unity. Cultural diversity must not be made an excuse for the lack of some visible demonstration of reconciliation and true oneness. Arguments for evangelizing "homogeneous units" must not undercut the biblical insistence on the unity of Christ's body.

*The structural principle for the expression of the unity of the Church is that of the body.* The Church is the body of which Christ is the only head. The principle of unity is the principle of many organs in one body. This principle holds good at every level of the Church. Thus, valid structures for unity must be based on a charismatic/organic model, rather than an institutional/hierarchical model. In practice, this means that such structures should be flexible and functional, and should be considered as para-church structures for the expression of oneness, not as an essential part of the Church itself.

*Priority should be given to the expression of Christian unity in to-day's urban centers.* Jacques Ellul suggests that "the city is man's greatest work. It is his great attempt to attain autonomy, to exercise will and intelligence."[15] The modern city is the battle-ground where the Church meets the principalities and powers. It is therefore the primary place where Christian unity needs to be demonstrated.

Wherever possible in cities around the world, large public rallies should be held regularly, uniting in the city all the people of God who will cooperate. If in major cities around the world all true Christians could unite regularly in a "great congregation" to joyfully sing praise to God, hear the Word and bear witness, the impact would be incalculable. Such rallies would give public, visible testimony to the unity of the body of Christ and put the Faith in the center of the public arena once again. These gatherings should be regular and frequent (probably once a month), and they should unite all who are willing to confess that Jesus Christ is Lord and Savior, whether Catholic, Protestant or Orthodox. They should be held in large public arenas wherever possible. Here the Church in each city could recover some sense of peoplehood that would cross denominational and confessional lines; and here the world could glimpse the visible reality of the unified Church.

*Some form of worldwide structure for unified fellowship and witness is necessary.* This structure should serve principally as (a) an information "nerve center" to monitor what is happening worldwide in the growth and witness of the Church; (b) a point of contact and communication between the many evangelical structures around the world, such as evangelistic-missionary structures, denominations, Bible societies, seminaries, colleges and the emerging evangelical communes; (c) an enabling structure or catalyst to bring about direct communication between similar structures in various parts of the world. Its function should be primarily one of information, communication and coordination, rather than one of initiating new programs of its own which would only tend toward institutionalism and the duplication of existing ministries.

If such a structure is based on a clear understanding of the Church, it will succeed in giving some visible, organized expression to the Church's unity without tending toward a superchurch. The structure must be essentially *para*-church rather than *super*-church. It must stand alongside and serve the true body of Christ, never being over it or appropriating to itself the prerogatives of the head, Jesus Christ. It will thereby promote a unity that is both spiritual and visible.

Evangelical Christianity today is more than a group of theologically conservative churches. It is decreasingly a specific branch of Western Protestantism and increasingly a transconfessional movement for biblical Christianity within the worldwide Church of Jesus Christ. It could become a worldwide movement providing hope for transcending

Western evangelicalism's bondage to American and European "culture Christianity."[16]

This is a time, however, not for triumphalism—evangelicalism's blemishes and tensions, both present and potential, are too serious for that—but rather for the emergence of what Donald Bloesch calls "a catholic evangelicalism." "The kind of theology that we should seek," says Bloesch, "is one that is both profoundly evangelical and authentically catholic." Biblically, "one cannot be fully evangelical without at the same time being truly catholic. And one cannot be catholic without also being evangelical."[17]

The time may be ripe around the world for the emergence of a thoroughly biblical evangelical movement that includes Catholic, Protestant, Orthodox and Jewish Christians. Arthur Glasser notes that "evangelical Protestants are beginning to encounter evangelical Catholics" and are discovering that "many loyal Catholics know and love Jesus Christ with an intimacy and devotion surpassing their own."[18] The biblical and charismatic emphases within Roman Catholicism in the wake of Vatican II are rapidly invalidating many traditional Protestant criticisms of the Roman Church. The charismatic movement already is bringing many Catholics and evangelicals together.[19] And in some countries where Catholics are experiencing renewal it is already an open question whether Catholics or Protestants are doing more evangelism.

The Covenant of the International Congress on World Evangelization is a nonsectarian document. It is, in fact, not even a specifically Protestant document. Because it sought to be both evangelical and biblical, it also succeeded in being surprisingly catholic. This Covenant, or something like it, could well serve as the basis for a worldwide Christian fellowship that is at the same time evangelical, catholic and charismatic.

Should these not, in fact, be the marks of evangelicalism's emerging unity in truth? For the Church of Jesus Christ must be *evangelical*—solidly based on the pure biblical gospel and its demands for witness and discipleship. The Church must also be *catholic*—concerned with the unity, universality and holiness of the Church. And it must also be *charismatic*—living in close community through the indwelling love, grace and power of the Holy Spirit as a present reality. It is thus that "the whole body, joined and held together by every supporting ligament, grows and builds itself up in love" (Eph. 4:16).

# EPILOGUE:
# FROM HERE
# TO THE KINGDOM

"From both our research and the feedback from the career missionaries whom we teach," writes Charles H. Kraft of the Fuller Seminary School of World Mission, "comes the overwhelming impression that one of the weakest plates in our theological armor is our doctrine of the Church. We tend either to talk about the Church in idealistic terms or to castigate the expressions of the Church around us because they don't measure up to the ideal. But we often seem to have little real understanding what is wrong or of any remedy for it, since theological approaches to the doctrine so largely ignore the cultural and sociological facets that constitute the majority of the overt features of 'churchness.' "[1]

In this book I have attempted to hold together the ideal and the real in that strange organism called "Church" and to align theological understandings with cultural and sociological realities, at least in a suggestive and rudimentary way. In this concluding section, as a further attempt to be practical and to speak of the Church in functional terms, I would like to offer seven suggestions for renewing the Church's authenticity and contributing to its kingdom vision.

**Seven Steps toward Renewal**    What can a local church do to increase its kingdom vision and become more authentically the community of the King?

1. *Undertake a study of the biblical nature of the Church.* Many local congregations could be revolutionized through a year-long study of the Church. Preaching and teaching could be coordinated with small-group Bible studies in which the Church is the main topic. The focus would be on such books as Acts, 1 Corinthians, Ephesians and Colossians, with attention given also to the Old Testament development of God's plan (particularly the concepts of the covenant and the people of God) and to the relevant material in the Gospels. Reading significant books on the Church should also be a part of this process. The bibliographical material at the end of this book gives some suggestions.[2]

All reading and other input, however, must be subservient to the study of the Scriptures and what they reveal about the Church and the Kingdom. My own thinking on the Church has benefited immeasurably from examining the Church in small-group Bible studies.

2. *Evaluate the quality of the community life of the church.* Some form of self-study—again using small groups—can be useful. The task of evaluation provides the objective focus, while small-group interaction deepens the personal experience of community. Lawrence Richards in *A New Face for the Church* gives guidelines for such evaluation, together with examples and illustrations.[3] Bible study should accompany evaluation.

3. *Attempt to think through what the Bible teaches about the gifts of the Spirit.* More heat than light radiates from this subject, but the biblical teachings are clear. Both pastoral and small-group emphasis on gifts (the two should go together) would focus on such passages as Romans 12, 1 Corinthians 12—14, Ephesians 4 and 1 Peter 4, with accompanying study of the related doctrine of the priesthood of believers. The aim would be to create a "gift consciousness" and help each believer

identify and use his or her gifts. The books *Full Circle, Body Life, Gifts of the Spirit* and *Handbook for Mission Groups* are quite helpful here (see bibliography).

4. *Attempt consciously to transcend the clergy-laity dichotomy in both thought and speech.* This seemingly frivolous suggestion is more substantial than it appears. Our speech patterns reflect and reinforce our concepts, and our concepts ultimately determine our actions. Awareness of nonbiblical language in speaking of the Church is as important as awareness of sexist or racist terms. Banning *layman* from one's vocabulary, for instance, forces a person to rethink his or her understanding of the Church and is a rewarding discipline. Further, small groups could study the biblical concepts of ministry and people, and begin to build their discoveries into their thought and speech. The goal is to remove any unbiblical dualism and create the awareness that all believers are God's people and have some "work of ministry." (In this book, *lay, laity* and *layman* are not used except in explanatory passages such as this one.)

5. *Consider forming one or two new congregations from the existing local church.* Some churches will never begin to grow until they divide. Churches of several hundred members should seriously consider gathering together a few families who live in the same area and using them as the nucleus of a new congregation. This is often more effective than preaching missions, "revival" campaigns or other intensive short-term efforts because it creates a second center of growth and deepens the involvement of all who participate.

This process of multiplication could be the natural outgrowth of the first three suggestions above. The new group formed does not immediately sever its connection with the mother church, but begins to carry on its own ministry and community life through small groups, service and worship. With sufficient growth, the group may have to move to a large basement or garage or other structure. It may rent a school, social hall or community center. By concentrating on people rather than programs or buildings, the group will soon be able to support one or more full-time workers. As normal church growth occurs, further division can take place.

6. *Form some small-group fellowships as mission or special-ministry groups,* as outlined in chapter eight. These groups can be especially effective for the church's social outreach. Gordon Cosby thoroughly explains one way such groups can function in *Handbook for Mission Groups.*

7. *Identify segments of the surrounding population especially open to the gospel where new churches could be planted.* Going one step beyond the fifth suggestion, a local church might actually seek out receptive groups within easy reach of the church and attempt to minister there. In urban centers, particularly, some church members will probably live near specific groups which may be highly receptive to the gospel. Such groups might include inner-city or outer-city poor, ethnic or occupational groups, or those institutionalized in hospitals, asylums or prisons and largely forgotten by society. Two or three families with the active support of the entire church could initiate an evangelistic ministry with the specific goal of planting a new self-supporting congregation. Melvin Hodges's little book, *A Guide to Church Planting,* provides excellent counsel for those wishing to begin a church-planting ministry.[4]

**The Cost of the Kingdom**   These suggestions do not mean that further fundamental innovations are not essential in the Church today. Our experience of the Church, by and large, still remains far too shallow. *Koinonia* for most of us is still either unperceived in its biblical dimensions or else remains an unattained vision we merely long for. We yearn to be open and honest and helpful and caring with our brothers and sisters and to have them be so with us. But the means to arrive at such a level of caring either elude us or appear too costly.

They would require us to open areas of our lives to others that we scarcely let even God peek into.

We must therefore learn from our Christian sisters and brothers of various communions who are now living and experiencing the deep sharing reality of the Church. In many cases we may find their practice at least as pure and biblical as our doctrine.

We should examine the new forms of Christian community springing up around us and, where necessary, initiate new patterns ourselves. Various forms of Christian communes or other intentional communities can help the larger church learn more fully the meaning of discipleship. They can show new ways of ministering to and incorporating the resources of the elderly and the institutionalized. They can furnish a home for Christian creative ministries in the arts, in writing and theological reflection.

The Kingdom of God in its fullness will probably not come tomorrow. Or next week. For the time being, more important than cocking an ear toward the skies for the trumpet call is listening carefully for the cries of the lost and the people without hope, and looking after the children too weak to cry because they have no food.

And certainly we should look to Jesus—risen, seated at God's right hand and sure to return. But we must also remember that Jesus walked this earth and died on the cross.

Think of Jesus on the cross. What does his suffering mean for us in this interim before the Kingdom fully comes? Should his body, the Church on earth today, be like he himself was two millennia ago?

Some say Christ suffered so we wouldn't have to. Jesus took our place on the cross and suffered there to save us. By his death we have life. Through his sorrow we have joy. By his self-emptying we are made rich.

But others look differently at the suffering of Jesus. They say his suffering reveals the dimensions of Christian discipleship. Christ's death and resurrection show us what happens to every person who seeks first the Kingdom of God. The crucifixion is a demonstration to us of the meaning and cost of discipleship. The cross, therefore, is not our escape from suffering, but rather our guarantee of suffering. Jesus is more our model than he is our route of escape.

Which view is biblical?

Both are. Jesus did take our place on the cross; through that sacrifice we have life. We have been made rich. "For you know the grace of our Lord Jesus Christ, that though he was rich, yet for your sakes he became poor, so that you through his poverty might become rich" (2 Cor. 8:9).

But that's not the whole story, and it's not the definition of discipleship. For Paul says, "Your attitude should be the same as that of Christ Jesus: Who, being in very nature God, did not consider equality with God something to be grasped, but made himself nothing, taking the very nature of a servant, being made in human likeness. And being found in appearance as a man, he humbled himself and became obedient to death—even death on a cross!" (Phil. 2:5-8). And John says, "In this world we are like him" (1 Jn. 4:17). Jesus said, "If anyone would come after me, he must deny himself and take up his cross daily and follow me" (Lk. 9:23). "Whoever claims to live in him must walk as Jesus did" (1 Jn. 2:6). And the apostle Peter tells us, "To this you were called, because Christ suffered for you, leaving you an example, that you should follow in his steps" (1 Pet. 2:21).

When we speak about our redemption, our eternal salvation, then we can joyfully say that Christ has suffered so we might not have to suffer. He has taken upon himself the guilt and punishment of sin. But when we speak of our life in the world, of discipleship, we see another truth at work. Scripture is consistent in showing that the disciple must be like his master and that self-denial, self-emptying and crucifixion are universal marks of those who follow Jesus.

But what kind of self-emptying? It is easy to have a distorted view of what the Bible means at this point. God is not asking us to reach down into our spiritual throats, yank out our own selfhood by the roots and cast it away. Real Christian faith is self-affirming, not self-mutilating. The true Christian does not try to get rid of his self or kill his will; rather he willfully determines to do the will of the Father. True discipleship is determining to do what Jesus showed his followers must do. Love for Christ means obedience to the Jesus lifestyle. When Paul said, "I am crucified with Christ," he was not describing an introspective psychological process by which he was reducing his ego to zero; rather he was saying, in effect, "I determine to give up my own rights just as Jesus did; I decide not merely to accumulate the benefits Christ has provided, but to follow his model in sharing these benefits with the world." Thus Paul says elsewhere, "I consider everything a loss compared to the surpassing greatness of knowing Christ Jesus my Lord, for whose sake I have lost all things. . . . I want to know Christ and the power of his resurrection and the fellowship of sharing in his sufferings, becoming like him in his death, and so, somehow, to attain to the resurrection from the dead" (Phil. 3:8, 10-11).

Kingdom ethics, therefore, is crucifixion ethics—life marked by the cross. It is the life laid down. And this runs counter to human nature. As humans, we prefer to substitute triumphal ethics for crucifixion ethics. We want to hurry on from the cross to the crown. We want to live now as though the Kingdom had already come in fullness; we prefer spiritually "to reign on earth." Through the centuries the Church has been tempted to act as though the Kingdom had already come, make peace with the world and settle down to comfortably enjoy the fruits of the gospel.

But then we get a glimpse of Jesus, trudging along through the dusk with his little band of disciples or wearily falling asleep in a rocking boat. Or we look up and see him stretched on a cross, fastened by three iron nails. His hands are wide open and the crown he wears is made of thorns.

True, we do not have to die on a cross. Jesus did that for us. And yet we are called to live crucifixion ethics. We are called to be cross-bearers more than cross-wearers. And the cross does not mean simply our sicknesses and our problems and the neighbor we cannot get along with. Rather the cross means voluntarily choosing to live our lives for others, letting the life of Jesus show us what true spirituality is.

During an informal, around-the-table discussion, a sweet, young Christian wife asked, "Is it wrong for Christians to enjoy nice things?"

Is it? No, of course not. Our eyes should be sensitive to beauty and excellence and harmony. Nor was it wrong for Jesus to enjoy nice things. It would not have been wrong for him to have been born in a palace or to have had expensive clothes, or to have dined sumptuously every day, for he is God and King and Lord.

But we come back to Philippians 2. Jesus was and is God but "he humbled himself and became obedient to death—even the death of the cross!" It is not wrong for us to enjoy nice things. But what would Jesus want us to do? It is not wrong for the Christian to have this world's goods—but John says, "If anyone has material possessions and sees his brother in need but has no pity on him, how can the love of God be in him?" (1 Jn. 3:17).

It is not wrong to have three meals a day and a roof over our heads. But what does Jesus think about those who have no roof over their heads and no meals any days? I confess that I become very uncomfortable when I hear Christians saying that since God has promised to give us "the desires of our hearts" we should therefore expect all kinds of "material blessings" from God. We may come to think that an ever-rising, middle-class standard of living is a kind of guaranteed minimum wage of the Christian faith, something that goes along with salvation. The theological implications of such a view are staggering. God is King, but if we think this means Christians are to live like royalty in a starving world then we should go back to the New Testament and take another look at the Jesus who preached the Kingdom.

Thank God for all the benefits we receive through Jesus' death on the cross! But let us thank him also for showing us the kind of life his followers are to lead; let us thank him for his Holy Spirit, given to enable us to live the life of discipleship by the values of the Kingdom.

The way to work effectively toward the Kingdom today is not primarily through emphasizing evangelism or social justice as things in themselves, but through the rediscovery of the Church as the community of the King. When the Church is the Church biblically understood, it grows and infects the world with an epidemic of health.

Kingdom witness and church growth are not a matter of bringing to the Church that which is needed for success in the way of methods, techniques or strategies. Kingdom faithfulness is a matter of removing the hindrances to life and growth. Once these hindrances (not only individual sin but also human traditions, worn-out structures and fundamental misconceptions about the nature of the Church) are removed, the Church will grow through the power of God within it.

When Lazarus was raised from the dead, he was "wrapped with strips of linen, and a cloth around his face." Jesus said, "Take off the grave clothes and let him go" (Jn. 11:44). This is a lesson for the Church today. The Church has resurrection life within it. It has been called to life by Jesus Christ (Eph. 2: 1-5). The body of Christ does not need a new suit of clothes. It does not need to have something added. It needs only to be unbound and let go.

Jesus Christ is life! The Church, his body and bride, is life! We need to return to God's Word and let it speak to us concerning the Church and its place in God's cosmic design.

The Church is the body of Christ, the community of the Holy Spirit, the people of God. It is the community of the King and the agent in the world of God's plan for the reconciliation of all things. God's agent of the Kingdom must not be considered just one means among many. For from the cross to eternity it remains true that "Christ loved the church and gave himself up for her to make her holy . . . and to present her to himself as a radiant church, without stain or wrinkle or any other blemish" (Eph. 5:25-27).

# Notes

## Introduction

[1]Marie-Dominique Chenu, *Nature, Man and Society in the Twelfth Century*, trans. Jerome Taylor and Lester K. Little (Chicago: University of Chicago Press, 1968), p. 240. Chenu points out that the aspiration to restore the Church to its primitive state "not only provoked a drive to moral reform, but also nourished a deep inquiry into the Christian faith that brought significant advances in theology" (ibid.). The two directions of this renewing thrust can be symbolized by the names of Francis and of Thomas Aquinas. So today the Church needs renewal both theologically and in its personal and corporate dimensions.

[2]Donald G. Bloesch, *The Evangelical Renaissance* (Grand Rapids: Eerdmans, 1973), p. 41.

[3]See Orlando E. Costas, *The Church and Its Mission: A Shattering Critique from the Third World* (Wheaton, Illinois: Tyndale, 1974), pp. 8-10, 21-57. Costas's analysis essentially parallels my own. He speaks of "the church as the agent of God's mission" but does not speak of this mission particularly in terms of the Kingdom of God.

[4]God's activity in the world is not confined to evangelical redemption; it also includes preservation and judgment. Thus God also acts outside the Church and even in judgment on the Church. But when it comes to redemption, the Church is the only agent God has chosen, that salvation may be by grace!

[5]Melvin L. Hodges, *A Guide to Church Planting* (Chicago: Moody, 1973), p. 15.

[6]Being a part of Christ means being part of his body. But the body of Christ must be understood biblically as the community of God's people, not primarily in terms of its institutional expressions.

[7]Jesus speaks of "the kingdom of God," "the kingdom of heaven," "my kingdom," "my father's kingdom," and so on. Although he perhaps intended some differences in emphasis, I do not believe Jesus intended any fundamental differences in meaning between the two phrases "kingdom of God" and "kingdom of heaven" (or, literally, "of the heavens"). Indeed, the two phrases may represent merely the preference of Matthew rather than differences in Jesus' usage.

[8]George Eldon Ladd, *Jesus and the Kingdom* (Waco, Texas: Word, 1964), pp. 42-43.

[9]Arnold A. Van Ruler, *The Christian Church and the Old Testament*, trans. Geoffrey W. Bromiley (Grand Rapids: Eerdmans, 1971), pp. 75-83.

[10]See Ladd, pp. 217-25. The English word *sacrament* traces back through the Latin to the Greek word *mustērion*. (See Edward Schillebeeckx, *The Mission of the Church*, trans. N. D. Smith [New York: Seabury Press, 1973], pp. 44-45.) While I do not deal with the sacraments in this book, any biblical discussion of sacraments would have to begin at this point.

[11]Marvin R. Vincent, *Word Studies in the New Testament* (New York: Charles Scribner & Sons, 1911), I, 311. For Ladd, the point of the parable of the leaven is that the Kingdom of God enters the world almost imperceptibly, not that the

Kingdom works like leaven to permeate society. But this is an unnecessary either/or argument; the point is both that the Kingdom begins hiddenly and that it gradually works to leaven the whole mass. Though Ladd feels the idea of permeation would have been "utterly foreign to Jewish thought," it is no more so than Jesus' teaching about the very nature of the Kingdom itself. See Ladd, *Jesus and the Kingdom*, pp. 232-34.

### Chapter 1

[1]Carl F. H. Henry, *Evangelicals in Search of Identity* (Waco, Texas: Word, 1976), p. 22.

[2]Carl F. H. Henry, *The Uneasy Conscience of Modern Fundamentalism* (Grand Rapids: Eerdmans, 1947), Preface.

[3]Ronald Nash, *The New Evangelicalism* (Grand Rapids: Zondervan, 1963); Millard Erickson, *The New Evangelical Theology* (Old Tappan, New Jersey: Revell, 1968); David O. Moberg, *The Great Reversal* (Philadelphia: Lippincott, 1972); David F. Wells and John D. Woodbridge, *The Evangelicals* (Nashville: Abingdon, 1975).

[4]Until 1976 *Sojourners* was called *The Post American*. While it is true that some younger evangelicals prefer to disassociate themselves from evangelicalism and therefore from the label *evangelical*, yet their historical linkage and their commitment to biblical authority (even if redefined) still place them within the broader context of contemporary evangelicalism. See especially Richard Quebedeaux, *The Young Evangelicals* (New York: Harper & Row, 1974) and *The Other Side*, 11:2 (March/April, 1975).

[5]Moberg, p. 177. See also Donald W. Dayton, *Discovering an Evangelical Heritage* (New York: Harper & Row, 1976).

[6]Sherwood Wirt, *The Social Conscience of the Evangelical* (New York: Harper & Row, 1968), p. 154.

[7]Carl F. H. Henry, *A Plea for Evangelical Demonstration* (Grand Rapids: Baker, 1971), p. 107.

[8]Leighton Ford, *The Christian Persuader* (New York: Harper & Row, 1966), p. 151.

[9]To avoid a universalist understanding of this "reconciliation of all things" one must bear in mind those Scriptures which speak of the judgment and eternal condemnation of Satan and of all who reject Christ, and the repulsion of all that is impure, unholy and false.

[10]The Lausanne Covenant may be considered one step in this direction (see chap. 2).

[11]Henry, *A Plea for Evangelical Demonstration*, p. 108.

[12]Ibid., pp. 113, 114.

[13]Francis A. Schaeffer, *Pollution and the Death of Man* (Wheaton, Illinois: Tyndale, 1968), p. 66.

[14]Ibid.

[15]Ibid., p. 67. For an excellent critique of Schaeffer's thought, see Thomas V. Morris, *Francis Schaeffer's Apologetics: A Critique* (Chicago: Moody, 1976).

[16]H. Richard Niebuhr, *The Kingdom of God in America* (New York: Harper Torchbooks, 1959), p. 135.

[17]Ibid., pp. 150-51.

[18]Ibid., p. 151.

[19]Harper & Row, 1976. Dayton outlines nineteenth-century evangelical involvement in and commitment to abolitionism, feminism, educational reform and concern to preach the gospel to the poor.

[20]See note 9, above.

[21]Many dispensationalists, of course, do not hesitate to map out a divine cosmic program, but this program has little place for human activity (except for the activity of sinners), and is discontinuous with space-time history.

[22]P. J. Hoedemaker, quoted in Van Ruler, *The Christian Church and the Old Testament*, p. 82.

## Chapter 2

[1]J. D. Douglas, ed., *Let the Earth Hear His Voice*, Official Reference Volume of the International Congress on World Evangelization (Minneapolis: World Wide Publications, 1975), pp. 3-9.

[2]The "radical discipleship" caucus was probably even more alert to the implications of the community/people terminology than were the participants generally. The adjectives *charismatic* and *messianic* in the paper "A Response to Lausanne" suggest themes which are especially congenial to the thrust of this book. See Douglas, *Let the Earth Hear His Voice*, pp. 1294-96.

[3]Henry Bettenson, ed., *Documents of the Christian Church* (New York: Oxford University Press, 1947), p. 298. Luther distinguished seven marks of the Church, all of which relate to the Word of God. The Church is marked by (1) the Word preached and believed, the Word symbolized and imparted through (2) baptism and (3) Holy Communion; the Word properly administered and safeguarded, which necessitates (4) ministers and (5) the office of the keys; (6) the Word used in worship; and the Word lived out, which is life marked by (7) the cross. All but the last of these relate fairly exclusively to the public worship of the Church.

Calvin's treatment of the marks of the Church is seemingly quite different from Luther's but in reality is quite similar. Repeatedly Calvin says there are two marks of the visible Church: the pure ministry of the Word and the pure celebration of the sacraments. "Wherever we see the word of God sincerely preached and heard, wherever we see the sacraments administered according to the institution of Christ, there we cannot doubt that the Church of God has some existence . . ." *(Institutes of the Christian Religion,* IV, i, 12). Here there are only two marks—or, if one separates the sacraments, three. But for Calvin the "proper administration" of the sacraments requires an ordained ministry and the necessity of the provision for excommunication. And the administration of the sacraments is a matter of public worship. So in essence there is no basic difference between Luther and Calvin as to how the Church on earth may be recognized.

One area of difference is that Calvin does not mention the cross or persecution as a mark of the Church. Calvin recognizes the place of the cross in Christian experience but apparently would not see persecution or suffering as a necessary mark. Luther mentions the cross although he puts it last on his list.

[4]E. Gordon Rupp, "The Doctrine of the Church at the Reformation" in *The Doctrine of the Church*, ed. Dow Kirkpatrick (Nashville: Abingdon, 1964), p. 73. Both Luther and Calvin believed, of course, that the Church was more than its visible expression. It was the people of God, the communion of the elect. But so far as its recognizable manifestation in space-time history was concerned, the emphasis (not exclusively, but primarily) was on proper teaching and order rather than on community or peoplehood.

[5]Bettenson, p. 350.

[6]See William R. Estep, *The Anabaptist Story*, rev. ed. (Grand Rapids: Eerdmans, 1975). Neither Luther nor Calvin saw the Church as identical with the state or with society in general. They even admitted a certain tension between the Church and society. But they did not conceive of the Church as a sociologically distinct, self-conscious community existing in evident tension with surrounding society, that is, as a counterculture.

[7]Avery Dulles, *Models of the Church* (New York: Doubleday, 1974).

[8]Peter Savage, "The Church and Evangelism," in *The New Face of Evangelicalism*, ed. C. René Padilla (Downers Grove, Illinois: InterVarsity Press, 1976), pp. 106-20.

[9]Dulles, p. 30.

[10]Cardinal Leon Joseph Suenens, *A New Pentecost?*, trans. Francis Martin (New York: Seabury Press, 1975), pp. 1-2.

[11]Ibid., pp. 2-3.

[12]Dulles, p. 27.

[13]There remain, obviously, fundamental and distinct differences between contemporary evangelical and Roman Catholic views of the Church. Many things in the ecclesiological statements of Vatican II are offensive to Protestants because they have very little explicit biblical basis. The point here is the question of primary emphasis.

[14]A somewhat parallel shift has occurred in that part of the church associated with the World Council of Churches. For a brief discussion, see Bernard Cooke, *Ministry to Word and Sacraments* (Philadelphia: Fortress Press, 1976), pp. 2-5.

[15]This is true, at least, for those who participated in the Lausanne Congress. A gathering of church administrators, rather than evangelistic leaders, might have come up with a different statement concerning the Church.

[16]Estep, p. 182.

[17]See pp. 110-12.

[18]See chap. 4.

## Chapter 3

[1]W. Robertson Nicoll, ed., *The Expositor's Greek Testament* (Grand Rapids: Eerdmans, 1961), III, 259. Thus our word *economic*. Note also the word *oikonomia* and its various translations in Ephesians 3:2; Colossians 1:25; 1 Timothy 1:4; Luke 16:2-4.

[2]Gerhard Kittel and Gerhard Friedrich, eds., *Theological Dictionary of the New Testament*, trans. G. Bromiley (Grand Rapids: Eerdmans, 1964-74), V, 151-52.

[3]Bernard Zylstra, quoted in *Perspective*, Newsletter of the Association for the

Advancement of Christian Scholarship, VII; 2 (March/April, 1973), p. 14.

[4]Note the recurrence of this significant phrase in Matthew 13:35; 25:34; John 17:24; Ephesians 1:4; Hebrews 4:3; 1 Peter 1:20; Revelation 13:8; 17:8. These passages make it clear that Christ was appointed as Savior from eternity and that God's kingdom plan is eternal.

[5]See Kittel and Friedrich, eds., *Theological Dictionary of the New Testament*, III, 681-82.

[6]A. A. Van Ruler, citing W. C. van Unnik, notes that the "Fathers use the word *mystērion* not only for the sacraments, but for all of God's action in history, the whole time filled by the Spirit in and from Jesus Christ. I think we should return to this broad and deep use of the term." *The Christian Church and the Old Testament*, pp. 78-79.

[7]Francis A. Schaeffer, *The God Who Is There* (Downers Grove, Illinois: InterVarsity Press, 1968), p. 152; *Pollution and the Death of Man*, pp. 66-69.

[8]John Bright, *The Kingdom of God* (Nashville: Abingdon Press, 1953), pp. 232-43.

### Chapter 4

[1]The phrase *through the church* is ambiguously translated "by the church" in the AV, thus masking the force of the fact that the Church is the *agent* of God's plan.

[2]See Avery Dulles, *Models of the Church.*

[3]The three points which follow are summarized from chap. 12 of *The Problem of Wineskins* (Downers Grove, Illinois: InterVarsity Press, 1975).

[4]Samuel Escobar, "Evangelism and Man's Search for Freedom, Justice, and Fulfillment," in Douglas, ed., *Let the Earth Hear His Voice*, p. 312.

[5]Hans Küng similarly describes the Church as "the People of God . . . the community of the faithful"; the Church is "the community of the new people of God called out and called together." *Structures of the Church,* trans. Salvator Attanasio (London: Burns and Oates, 1964), pp. x, 11.

[6]Küng, p. 12.

[7]Nicoll, III, p. 309.

[8]While still holding that the Church legitimately is an institution, a number of contemporary Catholic scholars admit, and even insist, that the charismatic/organic side of the Church must take precedence over the institutional. See, for example, Dulles, *Models of the Church.*

[9]David O. Moberg, *The Church as a Social Institution* (Englewood Cliffs, New Jersey: Prentice-Hall, 1962), p. 6.

[10]Ibid.

[11]See Geoffrey W. Bromiley, "The Charismata in Christian History," *Theology, News and Notes* (of Fuller Theological Seminary), Mar. 1974, p. 3.

[12]This affirmation is obviously not meant to justify any and all renewal movements, even if theologically orthodox. Many factors come into play in such cases, and each instance must be evaluated on its own merits.

[13]On the varied uses of the word *charismatic* see John Howard Yoder, "The Fullness of Christ," *Concern,* Feb. 1969, pp. 63-65.

[14]Bromiley, p. 24.

[15]The Church has no distinctive worth, of course, except as it bears the image of

God and is the recipient of God's grace and love.

[16]See pp. 112-14.

[17]In contrast, Satan's plan is to bring all things in heaven and earth under his own headship, or under the headship of a person or system which he controls.

[18]John Howard Yoder, *The Politics of Jesus* (Grand Rapids: Eerdmans, 1972), p. 63.

[19]See chap. 6 for further elaboration of the Church's kingdom tasks.

[20]These suggested criteria are derived from the whole tenor of the New Testament presentation of the gospel, and by deduction from such passages as Matthew 5:3-16; 1 Peter 2:11-17; Philippians 2:12-16; 1 Corinthians 10:31; John 13:35; Romans 12:3-21; 2 Corinthians 5:16-21, and others.

## Chapter 5

[1]John Howard Yoder, "A People in the World: Theological Interpretation," in *The Concept of the Believers' Church,* ed. J. L. Garrett, Jr. (Scottdale, Penn.: Herald Press, 1969), p. 259. The gospel is objectively true, regardless of the Church's unfaithfulness. But it can be betrayed and falsified before the world by the Church's disobedience.

[2]André Biéler comments, "Body and soul are co-equal; individuals and community are co-equal. A dualistic conception of man and his structure is a false division and an alienation of his true make-up. The Bible sends both materialists and spiritualists packing. Just as foreign to biblical thinking is a purely individualistic conception, isolating the individual from the community, or a collectivistic approach that would accord to the life of the community a privileged position over the individual." *The Politics of Hope,* trans. Dennis Pardee (Grand Rapids: Eerdmans, 1974), p. 35.

[3]Karl Barth, *Church Dogmatics,* trans. Geoffrey W. Bromiley (Edinburgh: T. & T. Clark, 1958), IV, 2, p. 627.

[4]The Authorized Version says, "As every man hath received the gift," implying that the gift of salvation is meant, but the Greek uses the word *charisma* here and has no definite article (see note 23 below).

[5]See chap. 11, "The Place of Spiritual Gifts," in *The Problem of Wineskins.* The best and most balanced practical discussion I have seen of spiritual gifts is *Gifts of the Spirit,* by Kenneth Kinghorn (Nashville: Abingdon, 1976).

[6]*Diakonon* in Romans 16:1 can be translated either "servant" or "deaconess" (as the NIV correctly notes). Phoebe's precise function is impossible to determine. See Kittel and Friedrich, *Theological Dictionary of the New Testament,* II, 93.

[7]Although the word *charisma* does not occur in this passage, the thought of "distributions of the Holy Spirit" suggests the author was speaking of the charisms.

[8]There is a striking parallel between 1 Peter 4:10-11 and Acts 6:2-4 (where Peter may well have been the spokesman). While the Acts passage is often thought of as "the institution of deacons," the noun for deacon does not occur. What we do have is "the ministry of the word" (*diakonia tou logou,* v. 4) and the ministry of "serving tables" (*diakonein trapedzais,* v. 2). This is parallel to the "If anyone speaks. . . . If anyone serves" distinction of 1 Peter 4:11.

[9]William Barclay, *The Letters to the Galatians and Ephesians* (Edinburgh: St. Andrew Press, 1966), p. 171. Biblically we probably should not, however, call these "office-bearers."

[10]Based primarily on Arndt and Gingrich, *A Greek-English Lexicon of the New Testament and Other Early Christian Literature* (Chicago: University of Chicago Press, 1957).

[11]Yoder, "The Fullness of Christ," pp. 33-93.

[12]Ibid., pp. 37-38.

[13]Ibid., pp. 38-39.

[14]Ibid., p. 39.

[15]Ibid.

[16]Ibid., p. 42.

[17]Ibid., p. 65.

[18]This same fluidity of vocabulary appears in the *Didache* (about A.D. 150), where *apostle* and *prophet* are used almost interchangeably and bishops and deacons are associated with the prophetic and teaching ministry.

[19]Note also the general, unspecified references in 1 Corinthians 9:5; 15:7; 17:9. *Apostles* seemingly has a broader meaning than the Twelve also in 1 Corinthians 15:3-7. Paul says the risen Jesus appeared first to Peter, "then to the Twelve," and later "to James, then to all the apostles."

[20]Watchman Nee argued that whereas the original twelve apostles were named by Jesus before his ascension, other apostles were designated by the Holy Spirit after Pentecost. Thus, *apostle* as spiritual gift in Ephesians 4 refers not to the Twelve but to those whom God designates through the Spirit during the age of the Church. See chap. 1 of *The Normal Christian Church Life* (Washington, D.C.: International Students Press, 1962). A strong case for the continuation of the apostolic ministry was made by B. T. Roberts in *Ordaining Women* (Rochester, New York: Earnest Christian Publishing House, 1891), pp. 79-85.

[21]The terminology used will make a practical difference, of course, in the way the apostle's role is perceived. For this reason some of the more heavily loaded ecclesiastical titles could to advantage be replaced by more functional ones (see note 23, below).

[22]Paul frequently emphasized his apostolic role and used it as a basis of his authority. It would be easy to conclude from this that Paul was basing his authority on the fact that he held the office of apostle. But his would be a misleading conclusion. Paul based his claim to authority precisely on the fact that he had been directly called and commissioned by God. For Paul, apostleship was not an office he filled but a calling and commission from God to which he had to be faithful. The authority was not extrinsic, based in the office, but was intrinsic, based on the call and continuing work of the Holy Spirit in Paul's own life. For Paul, apostleship and continuing faithfulness were inseparable.

[23]The truly biblical conception of ministry is often obscured in the Authorized Version because of the way some passages are translated. The modern reader should be aware that the same power structure which issued the King James Version in 1611 put two dissenters to death the same year for the threat they posed in holding that the Church should be separate from the State and that it

should be a believing community rather than a hierarchical institution. It is not surprising, therefore, that the AV reflects certain institutional/hierarchical assumptions not present in the original documents. One example is 1 Timothy 3:1, where the AV speaks of "the office of a bishop." The Greek does not have the word *office*; it merely says, "If anyone aspires to oversight" (*episkopes*). The New International Version correctly translates, "if anyone sets his heart on being an overseer," and the NEB says, "To aspire to leadership . . ." *Oversight* is to be preferred to *bishop* today, since ecclesiastical tradition has given *bishop* a specific hierarchical meaning completely foreign to the New Testament (compare note 4, above).

[24]To say that God has given the Church the prerogative to transfer or confer apostolic authority, so that an act of ecclesiastical authorities is ipso facto an operation of the Holy Spirit, rests on shaky biblical grounds and leads easily to an abuse of leadership roles.

[25]Barclay, p. 172. See also Green, *Evangelism in the Early Church*, pp. 168-69, 200-02; Eduard Schweizer, *Church Order in the New Testament* (London: SCM Press, 1961), p. 197.

[26]Kittel and Friedrich, *Theological Dictionary of the New Testament*, II, 736-37. Timothy apparently was not given the gift of an evangelist, although Paul exhorted him nevertheless to "do the work of an evangelist" as part of "the duties of your ministry" (2 Tim. 4:5). Evangelism was part of his ministry, but not his primary role.

[27]As Luther intimated in his sermon on Psalm 110:3, where he specifically relates the priesthood of all believers to the gifts of the Spirit:

Here the prophet applies the priestly office and adornment to the Christians, the people of the New Testament. He says that their worship of God is to consist in the beautiful and glorious priesthood of those who are always in the presence of God and perform nothing but holy sacrifices. . . .

Well, what is this "holy adornment," these priestly garments which adorn the Christians so that they become His holy priesthood? Nothing else than the beautiful, divine, and various gifts of the Holy Spirit, as St. Paul (Eph. 4:11, 12) and St. Peter (1 Peter 4:10) say, which were given to Christendom to advance the knowledge and the praise of God, a function which is carried out pre-eminently by the ministry of preaching the Gospel. . . .

. . . It is the Holy Spirit who adorns them in glory and holiness and clothes them in His power and with His gifts. (Commentary on Psalm 110. Jaroslav Pelikan and Helmut T. Lehman, eds., Luther's Works [Philadelphia: Fortress Press, and St. Louis: Concordia Publishing House, 1956-75], Vol. 13, pp. 294-95.)

This connection between the priesthood of believers and the gifts of the Spirit in Luther's thought has seemingly received very little attention. Yet without this emphasis Luther's doctrine of the priesthood of believers appears more static than he himself apparently conceived it to be. Luther saw the exercise of priestly functions within the Christian community as animated by the vivifying presence and ministry of the Holy Spirit. Note also Luther's comments on 1 Peter 4:10 in *Luther's Works*, Vol. 30, pp. 123-24.

In contrast Calvin scarcely mentions the priesthood of believers, sees the "royal priesthood" of 1 Peter 2:9 (a key verse for Luther) in rather static terms and particularly in terms of election and holds that "gifts are necessarily connected with offices." Calvin's strong emphasis on election caused him to see "the ministry of the Word" in terms of offices divinely instituted by an "inviolable decree." (See Calvin's commentary on 1 Peter 2:1-9 and on Ephesians 4:11.) Less emphasis is therefore placed on the gifts of the Spirit than one finds in Luther, and Calvin's view of ministry is therefore more rigid and suggests a greater clergy-laity distinction.

## Chapter 6

[1]Green, *Evangelism in the Early Church,* p. 48.

[2]Green notes, "The precise nature of this proclamation in the early church has been much discussed in recent years, particularly since the publication in 1936 of C. H. Dodd's *The Apostolic Preaching and Its Developments.* But there has been undue concentration on what has become technically known as the 'Kerygma,' which is supposed to have been a fairly fixed body of preaching material common to the early missionaries.... In the New Testament the *kērussein* root (to 'proclaim') is by no means primary. It is just one of the three great words used to refer to the proclaiming of the Christian message, the other two being *euaggelizesthai* (to 'tell good news') and *marturein* (to 'bear witness')." Green, p. 48.

[3]Ibid., p. 76.

[4]Gilbert James, address given to the third Continental Urban Exchange (CUE) Conference, Brooklyn, New York, February 26-27, 1976.

[5]See Yoder, *The Politics of Jesus.*

[6]C. Peter Wagner, *Frontiers in Missionary Strategy* (Chicago: Moody, 1971), pp. 124-34. See also Donald McGavran, ed., *Eye of the Storm* (Waco, Texas: Word, 1972), pp. 205-18.

[7]Some will perhaps say that anything which goes beyond producing conversions is no longer evangelism but becomes follow-up or nurture. The point is, however, that the evangelistic task is not really complete until it becomes self-perpetuating. Wagner comments, "Some regard follow-up as a separate step which comes after evangelism itself, but this is a fallacy all too common in evangelistic strategy." Jesus did not separate follow-up from evangelism. He included them all in the same package of "making disciples." Wagner, *Look Out! The Pentecostals Are Coming* (Carol Stream, Illinois: Creation House, 1973), pp. 45-46.

[8]Yoder, *The Politics of Jesus,* p. 113.

[9]Jacques Ellul, *The Presence of the Kingdom,* trans. Olive Wyon (New York: Seabury Press, 1967), pp. 9-11.

[10]Ibid., p. 10. Ellul states this in terms of the individual Christian; I would emphasize that this task is especially the function of the Church as the believing community of disciples.

[11]Ibid., p. 11.

[12]See *The Problem of Wineskins,* pp. 184-87.

[13]Quoted in Heinrich Bornkamm, *Luther's World of Thought,* trans. Martin

Bertram (St. Louis: Concordia, 1958), p. 130.

[14]Jesus is referring here to titles in the Church, not to the use of such terms as *father* or *teacher* in a functional sense. Thus the term *father* is rejected not in its literal sense within the home but as a title within the Church. The most appropriate titles within the Church are *brother* and *sister* because these are not titles but rather describe the true nature of the relationship of fellow believers in Christ.

[15]Jacques Ellul, *False Presence of the Kingdom,* trans. C. Edward Hopkin (New York: Seabury Press, 1972), pp. 107-08.

[16]Ibid., p. 15.

[17]See *The Problem of Wineskins,* chap. 3, "The Gospel to the Poor," pp. 37-53.

[18]Biéler, *The Politics of Hope,* p. 97.

[19]Ronald J. Sider, "Watching Over One Another in Love," *The Other Side,* 11:3 (May/June, 1975), p. 13.

**Chapter 7**

[1]Roland Allen, *The Spontaneous Expansion of the Church* (Grand Rapids: Eerdmans, 1962).

[2]See *The Problem of Wineskins,* especially chaps. 4, 5 and 6.

[3]Robert Webber, "Agenda for the Church, 1976-2000," *Eternity,* January 1976, pp. 15-17, 59-61.

[4]Green, *Evangelism in the Early Church,* p. 44. It is easy to point to the notable exceptions, both in the first century and later. Individuals of the intellectual and social elite were converted and became outstanding Christians. But the great majority of early believers, those who most readily accepted the gospel, were the poor masses.

[5]See *The Problem of Wineskins,* chap. 3, where I have dealt more fully with "the gospel to the poor."

[6]See George W. Peters, *Saturation Evangelism* (Grand Rapids: Zondervan, 1970), pp. 147ff.

[7]Neil Braun, *Laity Mobilized: Reflections on Church Growth in Japan and Other Lands* (Grand Rapids: Eerdmans, 1971), p. 21.

[8]See Peter Wagner's suggestion of a "celebration-congregation-cell" structure in larger churches (*Your Church Can Grow* [Glendale, California: Regal, 1976], pp. 97-109). Perhaps the first question in determining optimum size for a local congregation is, at what point would further growth require a major change in facilities, such as a new building? The key is to plan for planting one or more new congregations when the limit of present facilities approaches.

[9]Consider that Philip's encounter with the Ethiopian eunuch was a unique one-to-one situation, and that Paul's efforts in Athens were not remarkably fruitful. Philip's ministry in Samaria was dramatically successful numerically, but was weak at the very point of community until Peter and John arrived from Jerusalem. See Ray C. Stedman, *Birth of the Body* (Santa Ana, California: Vision House, 1974), pp. 131-40.

[10]See Carl Wilson, *With Christ in the School of Disciple Building* (Grand Rapids: Zondervan, 1976), especially chap. 12.

[11]Dr. Win Arn of the Institute for American Church Growth (Arcadia, California 91006) has produced a film, "Planned Parenthood for Churches," which effectively illustrates several of these points on church multiplication.

## Chapter 8

[1]One's theology of the Church must be derived predominantly from the Epistles and the Gospels, rather than from Acts. But Acts is the best source of information as to how the early church functioned and was structured.

[2]Christians today are in the remarkable situation of actually knowing more, at least potentially, about the early church and the first Christian centuries than any previous generation. This is due principally to twentieth-century discoveries and advances in archaeology, history, biblical studies and related fields. Those who take seriously the birth and life of the Christian Church as providing guidance for the Church today should be in the forefront of such research.

[3]Donald G. Bloesch, *Wellsprings of Renewal, Promise in Christian Communal Life* (Grand Rapids: Eerdmans, 1974), pp. 19-20. I am concerned, however, that Bloesch makes too easy demands on those not called to the more restrictive form of discipleship.

[4]A new study of St. Francis presenting varied perspectives on the twelfth-century saint is the anthology *Brother Francis,* ed. Lawrence Cunningham (Huntington, Indiana: Our Sunday Visitor, 1975). A recent fictionalized biography by a Protestant author is Glen Williamson's *Repair My House* (Carol Stream, Illinois: Creation House, 1973).

[5]Bloesch, p. 108.

[6]Ibid., pp. 108-12.

[7]See especially Ralph D. Winter and R. Pierce Beaver, *The Warp and the Woof: Organizing for Mission* (South Pasadena, California: William Carey Library, 1970), and Winter's "The Two Structures of God's Redemptive Mission," *Missiology,* 2:1 (January 1974), pp. 121-39.

[8]Winter and Beaver, *The Warp and the Woof,* p. 54.

[9]Ibid., p. 45.

[10]Winter terms these two structures *modality* and *sodality.* A modality is an entire church community, comprising whole families, while a sodality is a smaller community within the church with more restricted membership and dedicated usually to one specific task, such as missions or evangelism. See *The Warp and the Woof,* p. 52-62.

[11]Winter, "The Two Structures of God's Redemptive Mission," p. 121.

[12]Ibid., p. 122.

[13]Ibid.

[14]Ibid., p. 123. To the extent that these *ecclesiolae* or mission groups take on institutional forms, they become para-church structures, while the believers within them are no less the true Church. Wherever they are found or however they function, institutional ecclesiastical structures are best seen as para-church, not of the essence of the Church.

[15]Ibid., p. 124.

[16]Ibid., p. 126. The diocesan plan was borrowed from Roman political administra-

tion; Winter sees the monastic community as indebted to Roman military organization.

[17]Gordon Cosby, *Handbook for Mission Groups* (Waco, Texas: Word, 1975).

[18]These specific mission groups are only suggestive, of course. A local church, depending on its size, might have two or more groups involved with very specific social questions, such as drug abuse, abortion, child care or famine relief, rather than one catch-all "social reform fellowship." Likewise several groups might be involved with evangelism of different kinds. Groups arise out of a sense of need, so they will be as varied as the groups' gifts and as specific as the needs identified.

[19]Winter and Beaver, *The Warp and the Woof*, pp. 54-55.

[20]James F. Engel and H. Wilbert Norton, *What's Gone Wrong with the Harvest?* (Grand Rapids: Zondervan, 1975), especially pp. 79-102.

[21]David L. McKenna, "Drinking at a Shrinking Water Hole," *United Evangelical Action*, 34:4 (Winter 1975), p. 9.

[22]Jacques Ellul, *The Meaning of the City* (Grand Rapids: Eerdmans, 1970).

[23]Engel and Norton rightly suggest that "it is becoming increasingly apparent that a research department should be a part of any Christian communication organization, no matter how small" (p. 123). For further elaboration of Winter's "two structures" thesis, see Charles J. Mellis, *Committed Communities: Fresh Streams for World Missions* (South Pasadena: William Carey, 1976). For a conservative critique of the use of the term *para-church*, see four articles by James A. DeJong in *The Banner*, beginning with "Parachurch Groups: A Look at a New Term" in the June 10, 1977 issue (pp. 14-15).

**Chapter 9**

[1]Douglas, ed., *Let the Earth Hear His Voice*, p. 5.

[2]See Yehezkel Kaufmann, *The Religion of Israel*, trans. Moshe Greenberg (Chicago: University of Chicago Press, 1960).

[3]Second Vatican Council, *Decree on Ecumenism* (Washington, D. C.: National Catholic Welfare Conference, 1964), p. 1.

[4]See G. C. Berkouwer, *The Church*, trans. James E. Davison (Grand Rapids: Eerdmans, 1976).

[5]Küng, *Structures of the Church*, p. 12.

[6]Henri Blocher, "The Nature of Biblical Unity," in *Let the Earth Hear His Voice*, ed. J. D. Douglas, pp. 382-83.

[7]This affirmation is not meant to exclude the Jews, who in a special sense continue to be God's people.

[8]Peter Beyerhaus, *Shaken Foundations: Theological Foundations for Mission* (Grand Rapids: Zondervan, 1972), p. 42.

[9]C. René Padilla, "Evangelism and the World," in *Let the Earth Hear His Voice*, ed. J. D. Douglas, p. 131.

[10]"A Response to Lausanne," in *Let the Earth Hear His Voice*, ed. J. D. Douglas, p. 1294.

[11]Donald G. Bloesch, *The Reform of the Church* (Grand Rapids: Eerdmans, 1970), p. 184.

[12]Ibid., p. 186.

[13]It is well to remember that the modern ecumenical movement grew out of a genuine evangelistic and missionary concern. But with time it broke from its biblical and theological moorings and largely went astray. Because of this, many evangelicals practically equate ecumenism with heresy.

[14]C. Peter Wagner, *Frontiers in Missionary Strategy* (Chicago: Moody, 1971), pp. 153-60; Peters, *Saturation Evangelism*, pp. 76-77.

[15]Ellul, *The Meaning of the City*, p. 154.

[16]Younger evangelicals in North America, who have understandably and necessarily reacted against the theological narrowness and cultural bondage of much of American evangelicalism in their attempt to be radically biblical, need to be reminded that worldwide evangelicalism can no longer be defined solely by its North American expression. There are numerous emerging evangelical leaders in the Third World who share many of their concerns and perspectives and may have much to teach them.

[17]Bloesch, *The Reform of the Church*, pp. 186-87.

[18]Arthur F. Glasser, "The Evangelicals: World Outreach," in *The Future of the Christian World Outreach*, eds. William J. Danker and Wi Jo Kang (Grand Rapids: Eerdmans, 1971), p. 109.

[19]See Vinson Synan, *Charismatic Bridges* (Ann Arbor, Michigan: Word of Life, 1974).

**Epilogue**

[1]Charles H. Kraft, "Spinoff from the Study of Cross-Cultural Mission," *Theology, News and Notes* (of Fuller Theological Seminary), 18:3 (October 1972), p. 3.

[2]One must, however, guard against the danger of focusing too narrowly or exclusively on the Church. A study of the Church is often necessary because this has been a neglected area. But it is possible to go to the other extreme. A local church needs to understand the Church and God's plan for the Church. But then it needs to get on with the task of being the community of the King, and in its teaching it should cover the full range of emphases found in the Bible.

[3]Lawrence Richards, *A New Face for the Church* (Grand Rapids: Zondervan, 1970).

[4]See also Roger S. Greenway, ed., *Guidelines for Urban Church Planting* (Grand Rapids: Baker, 1976).

# Bibliography

The following bibliography is not exhaustive. It lists the principal publications mentioned in the book, as well as several others of particular significance which deserve comment. (See also the bibliography in *The Problem of Wineskins.*)

Allen, Roland. *The Spontaneous Expansion of the Church.* Grand Rapids: Eerdmans, 1962. First published in the thirties, this seminal work is still relevant to biblically-sound church growth.

Barclay, William. *The Letters to the Galatians and Ephesians.* Edinburgh: St. Andrew Press, 1966.

Berkouwer, G. C. *The Church.* Trans. James E. Davison. Grand Rapids: Eerdmans, 1976.

Bettenson, Henry. *Documents of the Christian Church.* New York: Oxford University Press, 1943.

Beyerhaus, Peter. *Shaken Foundations: Theological Foundations for Mission.* Grand Rapids: Zondervan, 1972.

Biéler, André. *The Politics of Hope.* Trans. Dennis Pardee. Grand Rapids: Eerdmans, 1974. Helpful on the Church's social role, but Biéler goes too far in the direction of economic and political "development" and sacrifices the uniqueness of the gospel.

Bloesch, Donald G. *The Evangelical Renaissance.* Grand Rapids: Eerdmans, 1973.

—————. *The Invaded Church.* Grand Rapids: Eerdmans, 1975.

—————. *The Reform of the Church.* Grand Rapids: Eerdmans, 1970. One of the better and more theologically substantial treatments of Church renewal. Excellent chapter on spiritual gifts in the Church.

—————. *Wellsprings of Renewal: Promise in Christian Communal Life.* Grand Rapids: Eerdmans, 1974. A provocative historical survey and contemporary overview of Christian intentional communities.

Braun, Neil. *Laity Mobilized: Reflections on Church Growth in Japan and Other Lands.* Grand Rapids: Eerdmans, 1971.

Chenú, Marie-Dominique. *Nature, Man and Society in the Twelfth Century.* Trans. Jerome Taylor and Lester K. Little. Chicago: University of Chicago Press, 1968. A mine of information about the medieval church, including a chapter on "The Evangelical Awakening" of the twelfth century.

Christenson, Larry. *A Charismatic Approach to Social Action.* Minneapolis: Bethany Fellowship, 1974. Shows the perspective in which the Church's social witness ought properly to be seen.

Cosby, Gordon. *Handbook for Mission Groups.* Waco, Texas: Word, 1975. A handbook for task- or mission-oriented small groups within the local church, based on the experience of Washington's Church of the Savior. Excellent.

Costas, Orlando. *The Church and Its Mission: A Shattering Critique from the Third World.* Wheaton, Illinois: Tyndale, 1974. A treatment of the Church which in many ways parallels my own.

Cunningham, Lawrence, ed. *Brother Francis: An Anthology of Writings by and about St. Francis of Assisi.* Huntington, Indiana: Our Sunday Visitor, 1972.

Danker, William J., and Wi Jo Kang, eds. *The Future of the Christian World Mission.* Grand Rapids: Eerdmans, 1971.

Dayton, Donald W. *Discovering an Evangelical Heritage.* New York: Harper & Row, 1976. A significant new study of the Church's social role in nineteenth-century America which raises questions for today.

Douglas, J. D., ed. *Let the Earth Hear His Voice.* Minneapolis: World Wide Publications, 1975. Some 1400 pages of papers and materials from the 1974 International Congress on World Evangelization.

Dulles, Avery. *Models of the Church.* Garden City, New York: Doubleday, 1974.

Durnbaugh, Donald. *The Believer's Church: The History and Character of Radical Protestantism.* New York: MacMillan, 1970.

Edwards, Gene. *The Early Church.* Goleta, California: Christian Books, 1974. Contains a number of helpful insights on apostleship and discipleship, but goes to an extreme in completely rejecting the institutional church.

Ellul, Jacques. *False Presence of the Kingdom.* Trans. C. Edward Hopkin. New York: Seabury Press, 1972.

——————. *The Meaning of the City.* Trans. Dennis Pardee. Grand Rapids: Eerdmans, 1970.

——————. *The Presence of the Kingdom.* Trans. Olive Wyon. New York: Seabury Press, 1967. Ellul's books are important for understanding contemporary culture and the Church's relation to it.

Engel, James F., and Norton, H. Wilbert. *What's Gone Wrong with the Harvest?* Grand Rapids: Zondervan, 1975. An excellent analysis of how churches can communicate effectively, and why they often do not. Attempts to take seriously the biblical nature of the Church. An important book.

Erickson, Millard. *The New Evangelical Theology.* Old Tappan, New Jersey: Revell, 1968.

Estep, William R. *The Anabaptist Story.* Rev. ed. Grand Rapids: Eerdmans, 1975.

Ford, Leighton. *The Christian Persuader.* New York: Harper & Row, 1966.

Garrett, James Leo, Jr., ed. *The Concept of the Believers' Church.* Scottdale, Pennsylvania: Herald Press, 1969.

Gish, Arthur. *Beyond the Rat Race.* Scottdale, Pennsylvania: Herald Press, 1973. Thought-provoking material on carrying the implications of the gospel through to practical areas of life. Helpful for rethinking discipleship in the Church.

Green, Michael. *Evangelism in the Early Church.* Grand Rapids: Eerdmans, 1970. A scholarly but readable account based on original research. Very helpful in understanding the early church.

Greenway, Roger S., ed. *Guidelines for Urban Church Planting.* Grand Rapids: Baker, 1976.

Hardesty, Nancy, and Scanzoni, Letha. *All We're Meant to Be.* Waco, Texas: Word, 1975. This attempted biblical approach to Christian feminism raises issues which must be dealt with in any genuine Church renewal today.

Henry, Carl. *The Uneasy Conscience of Modern Fundamentalism.* Grand Rapids: Eerdmans, 1947.

_____. *Evangelicals in Search of Identity.* Waco, Texas: Word, 1976.

_____. *A Plea for Evangelical Demonstration.* Grand Rapids: Baker, 1971.

Hodges, Melvin. *A Guide to Church Planting.* Chicago: Moody, 1973. Helpful insights from one who contributed much to the "indigenous church" concept. Although based on foreign missionary experience, many of the insights are widely applicable and are compatible with the biblical view of the Church.

Hudnut, Richard. *Church Growth Is Not the Point.* New York: Harper & Row, 1975.

Kaufmann, Yehezkel. *The Religion of Israel.* Trans. Moshe Greenberg. Chicago: University of Chicago Press, 1960.

Kinghorn, Kenneth C. *Gifts of the Spirit.* Nashville, Tennessee: Abingdon, 1976.

Kingsley, Charles W. *Do.* Winona Lake, Indiana: Light and Life Men International, 1976. Gives strong evidence for the Church's evangelistic mandate by emphasizing "contrasts" between the New Testament church and the church today.

Kittel, Gerhard, and Friedrich, Gerhard, eds. *Theological Dictionary of the New Testament.* Trans. Geoffrey Bromiley. Grand Rapids: Eerdmans, 1964-74.

Kirkpatrick, Dow, ed. *The Doctrine of the Church.* New York: Abingdon, 1964. A collection of essays prepared under the direction of the World Methodist Council.

Kraemer, Hendrik. *A Theology of the Laity.* Philadelphia: Westminster Press, 1958. A very significant, seminal study of the true meaning of "laity."

Küng, Hans. "The Charismatic Structure of the Church." In *The Church and Ecumenism*, Vol. 4 of *Concilium*, ed. Hans Küng. New York: Paulist Press, 1965, pp. 41-61. An excellent discussion emphasizing that "to rediscover the charismata is to rediscover the real ecclesiology of St. Paul."

_____. *The Church.* Garden City, New York: Image Books, Doubleday, 1976.

_____. *Structures of the Church.* Trans. Salvator Attanasio. London: Burns and Oates, 1964.

Ladd, George Eldon. *Jesus and the Kingdom.* Waco, Texas: Word, 1964.

McGavran, Donald. *Eye of the Storm.* Waco, Texas: Word, 1972.

Moberg, David O. *The Church as a Social Institution.* Englewood Cliffs, New Jersey: Prentice-Hall, 1962.

_____. *The Great Reversal: Evangelism Versus Social Concern.* Philadelphia: Lippincott, 1972.

Nash, Ronald. *The New Evangelicalism.* Grand Rapids: Zondervan, 1963.

Nicoll, W. Robertson, ed. *The Expositor's Greek Testament.* Grand Rapids: Eerdmans, 1961.

Niebuhr, H. Richard. *The Kingdom of God in America.* New York: Harper Torchbooks, 1959.

Padilla, René, ed. *The New Face of Evangelicalism: An International Symposium on the Lausanne Covenant.* Downers Grove, Illinois: InterVarsity Press, 1976. A discussion of a number of issues raised at Lausanne, 1974.

Peters, George. *Saturation Evangelism.* Grand Rapids: Zondervan, 1970.

Quebedeaux, Richard. *The Young Evangelicals: Revolution in Orthodoxy.* New York: Harper & Row, 1974.

Richards, Lawrence. *A New Face for the Church.* Grand Rapids: Zondervan, 1970. One of the more comprehensive and balanced treatments of contemporary church renewal to be written by an evangelical. Includes a number of practical aids toward both structural and personal renewal.

Roberts, Benjamin Titus. *Ordaining Women.* Rochester, New York: Earnest Christian Publishing House, 1891. This Christian feminist tract includes a good treatment of the biblical understanding of ministry.

Schaeffer, Francis A. *The God Who Is There.* Downers Grove, Illinois: InterVarsity Press, 1968.

_____. *Pollution and the Death of Man.* Wheaton, Illinois: Tyndale, 1970.

Schweizer, Eduard. *Church Order in the New Testament.* London: SCM, 1961. A scholarly study with much useful information, but based on questionable presuppositions as to how forms of church order developed historically.

Schillebeeckx, Edward. *The Mission of the Church.* Trans. N. D. Smith. New York: Seabury Press, 1973.

Second Vatican Council. *Decree on Ecumenism.* Washington: National Catholic Welfare Conference, 1964.

Snyder, Howard A. *The Problem of Wineskins: Church Structure in a Technological Age.* Downers Grove, Illinois: InterVarsity Press, 1975.

Stedman, Ray C. *Birth of the Body.* Santa Ana, California: Vision House, 1974. An Exposition of the first part of Acts; not as helpful for understanding the Church as *Body Life.*

_____. *Body Life.* Glendale, California: Regal, 1970. Excellent on the functioning of the local church as Christ's body.

Suenens, Leon Joseph, Cardinal. *A New Pentecost?* Trans. Francis Martin. New York: Seabury Press, 1975.

Synan, Vinson. *Charismatic Bridges.* Ann Arbor, Michigan: Word of Life, 1974.

Van Ruler, A. A. *The Christian Church and the Old Testament.* Trans. Geoffrey W. Bromiley. Grand Rapids: Eerdmans, 1971.

Wagner, C. Peter. *Frontiers in Missionary Strategy.* Chicago: Moody, 1971.

_____. *Look Out! The Pentecostals Are Coming.* Carol Stream, Illinois: Creation House, 1973.

Wallis, Jim. *Agenda for Biblical People.* New York: Harper & Row, 1976.

Wells, David F. and Woodbridge, John D., eds. *The Evangelicals.* Nashville, Tennessee: Abingdon, 1975.

Wilson, Carl. *With Christ in the School of Disciple Building.* Grand Rapids: Zondervan, 1976. An important new book on discipleship.

Winter, Ralph D. "The Two Structures of God's Redemptive Mission." *Missiology,* 2:1 (January, 1974), pp. 121-39.

Winter, Ralph D., and R. Pierce Beaver. *The Warp and the Woof: Organizing for Mission.* South Pasadena, California: William Carey Library, 1970.

Wirt, Sherwood. *The Social Conscience of the Evangelical.* New York: Harper & Row, 1968.

Yoder, John Howard. "The Fullness of Christ, Perspectives on Ministries in

Renewal." *Concern*, No. 17 (February, 1969), pp. 33-93.
_____. *The Politics of Jesus*. Grand Rapids: Eerdmans, 1972. A basic book for rethinking Christian discipleship and the nature of the Church today.